C000054506

A GRIM ALMANAC OF

NOTTINGHAMSHIRE

An ACCOUNT of the LIVES, TRIAL, and BEHAVIOUR of

William Wainer and James Brumage,

Who were executed on NOTTINGHAM Gallows, on Wednesday the 30th of July, 1766, For a Foot-Pad-Robbery; with the genuine Confession of the latter, as deliver'd himself.

AT the Assizes for the County of Nottingham, held on Monday the 14th of July, 1766, before the Rt. Hon. Lord Camden, Lord Chief Justice of the Common Pleas, William Wainer and James Brumage, were indicted for robbing Mr. John Hall, (servant to Mr. Trotter Register at Durham) of thirty-two shillings in gold and silver, and after a fair trial, in which they behaved with great boldness, were capitally convicted, and received sentence of Death.—His Lordship previous to his passing sentence upon the prisoners, in a most pathetic speech, earnestly exhorted them to prepare seriously for another World, for their crimes had been so notorious, as rendered them improper objects of mercy, and they must fall a sacrifice to public justice.—This seasonable advice, made great impression on the minds of the unhappy youths, particularly Brumage, who in good earnest resolved to make the best use of the short time he had to live, and begged the assistance of a worthy divine; but Wainer declared himself a papist; refused to attend the service of the Church, and requested the aid and assistance of a Catholic Priest; who, it is said, finding him but little acquainted with the doctrines of the church of Rome, was not forward to attend him, and neglecting to visit him for several days, Wainer was prevailed on to accompany his fellow prisoner to church, where he behaved with decency, and seemed resolved to die in the Protestant religion; but the Thursday before he suffered, the priest paid him another visit; and then Wainer declared his final resolution to die in the communion of the church of Rome.—He obstinately refused to make any confession, but to God, the Saints, and the Priest, and was very angry with Brumage for endeavouring to persuade him, nor would he give any account of his late past life, tho' much urged by the worthy goaler and others: The Printer therefore, can say no more of him than giving the following short history of his life, gathered from the conversation of those who knew him.

WILLIAM WAINER, aged about 23 years, was born at Roulston, near Newark in Nottinghamshire; his father rented a small farm there and had several children; William was put apprentice at 12 years of age, to a Framework-knitter, at Woodborough, where he behaved well, and was a constant frequenter of the church of England; after his time was expired, he lived with Mr. Harris, a hosier in Nottingham, about three years; here he behaved tolerably well, but falling in love with his master's daughter, and she on account of some irregularities prudently refusing his addresses, he went to Coventry, and was employed by Mr. Clay, as a servant in the manufactory of that city. He declared to a friend, that passing over Nottingham

meadows, when he set out first for Coventry, he then was determined never to return into Nottinghamshire, unless it was to be hanged; for that he could not be happy again, nor did he care what course of life he led—Strange as this absurd resolution may appear, it was but too soon put into practice, for he had not been long in the service of Mr. Clay, before he was violently suspected of defrauding his master, of divers parcels of silk, and was committed to goal, but at the last Lent Assize, acquitted for want of evidence: How he spent his time after his discharge from prison will appear by reading the following annexed confession of James Brumage, whose whole behaviour has been very different from that of Wainer, being patiently resigned to his approaching change, behaving in every respect as became one in his unhappy circumstances, and at last dying with a truly christian fortitude, desiring the prayers of all present, and departing this life in the 22d year of his age:

I James Brumage, being in a few hours to suffer a shameful death, and appear before that God to whom all secrets are open, think it my duty before I launch into eternity, to give this following genuine account of my life and actions, to ease my conscience, and clear such innocent persons who may be suspected of those crimes, I or my wicked companions were guilty of:

I was born at Willoughby, in Warwickshire; my father was a publican there and had 5 children, which he endeavoured to bring up to business in a creditable manner; but providence deprived us of our dear Parents, when I was just ten years old; my mother was buried one Sunday, my brother the next, and my father the Sunday following, in the year 1755; thus we lost three dear relations within fifteen days of each other, who left me, and four other children orphans. My father on his death bed, requested Mr. Bonnington a butcher of the same town, his friend, to take care of his children and effects, which he promised to do: A little before he expired, I being his favourite child, he sent for me to his chamber, and bid me take care of a leather purse, which he took from under his pillow, and gave into my hand (which purse contained about 45l.) with a strict charge to tell nobody. Soon after my poor father's death, Mr. Bonnington took possession of the house and business, but proved a careless man, and tho' I was very young, I thought it better to keep the money than give it him: In about one year after, he died, but in that short time wasted the greatest part of my Father's substance, and tho' there was a few valuable effects ill left, which if properly applied, might have afforded some relief to us poor children, for want of a will, which my father should have made, all was lost; however, some kind

A GRIM ALMANAC OF
NOTTINGHAMSHIRE

KEVIN TURTON

First published 2005
This edition published 2009

The History Press
The Mill, Brimscombe Port
Stroud, Gloucestershire, GL5 2QG
www.thehistorypress.co.uk

© Kevin Turton, 2005, 2009

The right of Kevin Turton to be identified as the Author
of this work has been asserted in accordance with the
Copyrights, Designs and Patents Act 1988.

All rights reserved. No part of this book may be reprinted
or reproduced or utilised in any form or by any electronic,
mechanical or other means, now known or hereafter invented,
including photocopying and recording, or in any information
storage or retrieval system, without the permission in writing
from the Publishers.

British Library Cataloguing in Publication Data.
A catalogue record for this book is available from the British Library.

ISBN 978 0 7524 5593 8
Typesetting and origination by The History Press
Printed in Great Britain

CONTENTS

Mansfield Cemetery.

ACKNOWLEDGEMENTS

I am indebted to the following, without whom this book would never have been completed, let alone packed with so many grim tales of the past: the staff of Nottingham Local Studies Library, who pointed me in the right direction and gave me access to information I never realised existed, the coffee-bar team on the second floor who kept me going with copious cups of tea and provided a hot lunch when it was so desperately needed; Newark Library, where nothing was ever too much trouble and the staff were tireless in their help; Mansfield Local Studies Library, where access to information was never a problem and where local knowledge proved invaluable; and lastly the hundreds of newspaper reporters who, over the last three centuries, meticulously recorded the events of daily life that so enthralled the readership of the *Newark Advertiser*, the *Nottingham Journal* and the Nottingham Eve*ning Post*. Without them many of the stories recorded here would never have seen the light of day and investigative writers like myself (and others before and since), would have found our research all the more arduous. Of course I also have to thank those archivists of the past who had the foresight to realise that newspapers would have such a real and necessary place in history. In previous centuries, of course, it was considered necessary for journalists to record detail in great depth, allowing us much more than a glimpse into history. So intense are the feelings invoked in me when I read of an event from the dim and distant past that I feel the ghosts stirring, particularly where they suffered some great tragedy. For a brief moment, in my mind's eye, the people whose lives I write of live again, albeit briefly, and the past, no matter how bizarre, macabre, murderous or grim, becomes very real. Each and every personal event recorded in this almanac is true. The people who populate this book lived and breathed their way through the centuries, their anonymity stripped away by an army of scribes whenever their lives entered the public arena.

My thanks also go to the many authors past and present whose work has aided my own. They include *John Darrell The Nottinghamshire Exorcist* by Frank Earp; *Mansfield in the Eighteenth Century* and *Historic Mansfield* by A.S. Buxton; *Facts and Fictions* by John Potter Briscoe; *A Nottinghamshire Christmas* by John Hudson; *A History of Newark On Trent* by Cornelius Brown; *Nottinghamshire in the Civil War* by Alfred C. Wood; *Brothers at War* by Robin Brackenbury; *The Nottingham Date Book, Of Bridles and Burnings* by E.J. Burford and Sandra Shulman; *The Encyclopaedia Of Executions* by John

J. Eddleston; *The Art of Mystery and Detective Stories*, by Peter Haining; and *Ghosts and Legends of Nottinghamshire*, by David Haslam.

Every attempt has been made to trace and contact the original owners of all images used in this book where relevant. If copyright has inadvertently been infringed, copyright holders should write to the publishers with full details. Upon copyright being established, a correct credit will be incorporated into future editions of the book. All pictures are from the author's collection unless otherwise stated.

Mansfield Cemetery.

INTRODUCTION

The enduring popularity of crime, murder and all things grim is one of the indisputable features of literature past and present. People have always held a particular fascination for the genre that creates mystery and mayhem. Since the days of the penny broadsheets sold at public executions to eager crowds of spectators, the public at large has almost always thrilled to stories about the darker side of life. Murder, manslaughter, witchcraft and the macabre have formed the basis of some of the best-selling novels in history, and when fact mimicked fiction people often took to the streets, filled the courtrooms and jostled in front of public scaffolds. Whether we like it or not, a part of the human psyche seems unable to condemn and ignore the evil side of human nature which we know to be wholly unacceptable to any civilised society. Perhaps it is that very fact that creates the fascination. We know it should never happen, but we also know that it does and because it does, we want to understand it better. We seem to have a voracious appetite for all things criminal and if a story errs on the side of the ghoulish then so much the better. If it were the opposite, of course, we would never have followed the exploits of Sherlock Holmes or delved into the mind of Edgar Allan Poe, and would never have watched *The Exorcist* at the cinema.

History records that this is nothing new, and confirms that there is nothing sinister about us as human beings. It has been going on for centuries but probably developed in a literary sense during the Victorian period, when society was obsessed by crime and justice – though some of that justice was rough in the extreme. Penny dreadfuls, penny bloods, the *Police Gazette*, broadsheets newspapers giving comprehensive coverage of murder trials, the last letters of the condemned and the final confessions of those about to die were gobbled up by an eager public. Our sensibilities may have changed – we are no longer Victorian in outlook and our views on crime and punishment have certainly developed – but our curiosity about all things evil has not.

Thousands upon thousands have visited Madame Tussaud's famous waxworks since it opened in 1835 but not just to see the faces of the famous. Many visitors were equally fascinated by the images of notorious murderers and the dark terrors of the Chamber of Horrors. Thousands more have read the numerous books that have been written about some of Britain's most infamous men, while Hollywood has created its own library of all things grim and grisly. Fame, it seems, is often granted to those who perpetrate the most

Mansfield Cemetery.

deviant acts of violence, although not to the executioners who (until 1964) enforced the penalty of the law.

In 1924 John Ellis retired without a pension. He had been Britain's executioner for twenty-three years, and had taken part in 203 executions. The man who had stood on the scaffold with Dr Hawley Harvey Crippen in November 1910 was shunned by the government that had employed him. Despite his role in society he was relatively unknown outside his native Rochdale, where he ran a barber's shop. He became more a source of curiosity than celebrity. People wanted to know of him but not necessarily about him. They would visit his shop, invite him to give lectures and flock to his seaside town demonstrations of the British method of execution. But of his life, both past and present, they knew very little and asked even less. So when he committed suicide in September 1932, at the age of fifty eight, it was perhaps not unexpected. What ought to have been remarked upon was the fact that neither the Home Office nor the Prison Commissioners sent a representative to his funeral.

In my research over the years I have often thought how bizarre it is that men like Ellis never really received any recognition. Their names are often known – Calcraft, Billington, Baxter, Pierrepoint – but little else, and I have come to the conclusion that perhaps that is how it ought to be. Notoriety is reserved for the criminal, while anonymity should protect and conceal those who operate the mechanism of the law.

We want to explore the causes, the motives, the people and the events that led up to those dark and deadly deeds that populate our murky past – and the more mysterious and sinister the better. We want to know about witches and warlocks, riots, disasters, unusual funerals, notable lives, execution and murder. The more extraordinary the behaviour, the more our interest is aroused.

This, of course, was realised many years ago and seized upon by authors such as Wilkie Collins, who created the first truly atmospheric mystery in his novel *The Woman in White*. Charles Dickens used it to great effect in *Barnaby Rudge*, and Edgar Allan Poe in 'The Murders in the Rue Morgue'

From this came the detective figure, the man who solved the most baffling of crimes. Everyone is familiar with Sherlock Holmes, the fictional character who far outshone his creator, but there have been many others. Since the early nineteenth century writers have been creating stories populated by fictional characters whose job it was to uncover some dreadful murderer or solve an impossible crime. Many of these authors, whose names are long since forgotten, threaded real crimes into their narratives, which added realism to their stories and captivated a willing readership. As the years went by readers became more discerning and, as television replaced books, demanded ever more realism. Fiction, therefore, has now begun to mirror truth perhaps in more ways than it ever did in the past.

This book therefore is a journey through a collection of truths, a journey that, no matter how bizarre or gruesome, is as enlightening as it is engrossing. The people in the following pages all lived. No fiction embellishes the facts and every story, whether gruesome, bizarre, macabre or strange, is true. This is why Robin Hood, perhaps Nottingham's most famous citizen, is not to be found here. This omission is deliberate, not because he has no place in Nottingham's rich past but simply because I could find no dark and sinister side to the man. So I apologise in advance to any that seek him here; his past has been far too well guarded to be uncovered now and is perhaps best left hidden by the misty wreaths of time.

This 'Grim Almanac' is the product of many hours of research, during which I have thumbed my way through numerous archives covering murder, execution, coroners' reports and some sensational newspaper reportage. In a comprehensive investigation I have blown away the dust of centuries to reveal Nottingham's dark and sinister past. Each day in this almanac exposes a grim story from the county's murky past, rarely spoken of and hardly ever published. This is your chance to meet some of those who peopled that past. I hope you enjoy the journey – and above all have a good read.

JANUARY

Trent Bridge, Nottingham, *c.* 1930.

1 JANUARY **1842** The inquest opened at Mansfield into the death of Mary Hallam, aged 20. Her body had been discovered by her own father inside the workshop of a man he knew as Samuel Moore. She was lying on the floor in front of an open fire. Her throat had been slashed open some hours earlier and according to medical opinion she had died almost instantly. Moore, a shoemaker, was later found drinking in a nearby pub and freely admitted his guilt. He told the arresting police officers that he had fallen in love with Mary and had invited her to see his workshop. She, he insisted, had readily agreed and had arrived that evening at around 6 p.m. The two spent some time alone and Moore asked her to marry him. She refused and in a fit of jealous rage he had attacked her with a shoemaker's knife. In a statement presented to the coroner's court he had also told police that having committed the murder he contemplated suicide, but after debating the issue with himself he had decided that if he killed himself then he would have to atone for two sins when he stood before God, murder and suicide. He therefore decided instead to await capture and accept the court's decision. The jury had no doubt as to his guilt and the coroner, Mr Shaw, concurred. A remorseful Samuel Moore, whose real name was John Jones, stood in the dock three months later charged with wilful murder and after a brief hearing was declared guilty a second time. Penitent, he mounted the scaffold in front of Nottingham's County Hall on 23 March and at precisely 25 minutes to 9 in the morning was launched into eternity before a huge crowd of eager onlookers.

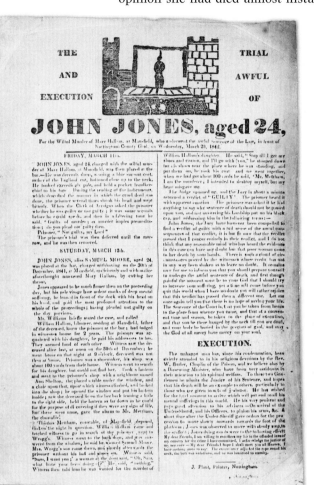

Above: An account of the trial and execution of John Jones, alias Samuel Moore, who murdered Mary Hallam.

2 JANUARY **1806** Excited reports circulated throughout the city on this day after it became known that a duel with pistols had been fought at Basford, Nottingham, between Lieutenant Browne of the 83rd Regiment of Foot, a young man of only 17, and Ensign Butler of the 36th Regiment of Foot, both of whom had been on recruitment service in Nottingham. They fired their pistols and the young lieutenant fell to the ground mortally wounded. He was carried into Basford's parish church where he later died. His body was brought back to Nottingham and interred in St Mary's churchyard. A detachment of the 3rd Dragoons attended the funeral and formed up around the grave to fire three volleys into the air as a mark of respect.

1689 Churchwardens at Mansfield Woodhouse ordered that 22-year-old Mary Thornton be publicly whipped for begging and then forced to return to her home in Yorkshire within twelve days or suffer a repeat of the punishment.

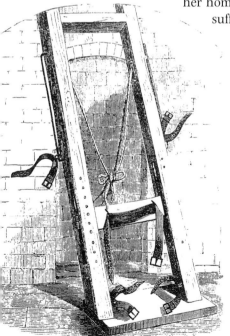

A whipping post.

1832 John Armstrong (aged 26) and Thomas Shelton (38) were both sentenced to be hanged after being found guilty of causing a riot in Beeston in December 1831. The men, apparently at the head of some 3,000 rioters, had been seen setting fire to William Lowe's silk mill, which burnt to the ground as a result. Thomas Shelton, it also transpired, had played a prominent part in earlier rioting at Colwick, which had resulted in a house being robbed of jewellery. The jewellery in question was recovered from a Nottingham jeweller who had identified Shelton in court as the man who had sold it to him.

5 JANUARY   **Old Nottinghamshire Beliefs and Sayings** If a girl has two lovers and wishes to know which of them would be more faithful, she must take two brown apple pips and stick one on each cheek of her face. Then she must name the two lovers out loud and repeat:

> Pippin, Pippin, I stick thee there,
> That that is true thou mayst declare.

She must then wait patiently until one falls off, thus indicating which lover she must discard.

6 JANUARY   **1892**   An inquest opened at the Newcastle Arms Inn, Southwell, into the death of an unknown man. Found lying on the railway lines near Southwell, he had clearly been struck by a train that had shattered his right hand and severely bruised his head. According to railway experts the injuries he had sustained were consistent with his having been lying between the lines and run over, probably by the 6.28 p.m. train to Mansfield. There was a 15in gap between the train and the ground, and the man must have lain inside that space, otherwise his body would have been very badly mangled. The bruising to his head was consistent with his having attempted to sit up as the train ran over him. The man's identity was never discovered.

7 JANUARY   **1884**   A report in the *Newark Advertiser* told the appalling story of 15-year-old Sarah Ann Leach. After running away from her employers she surrendered herself to Newark police, who discovered after a medical examination that she had been severely mistreated over a protracted period of time. In addition to being seriously emaciated, she had four deep scalp wounds, both her thighs were covered with long weals indicating she had been whipped, her nose was badly swollen from being punched, her mouth was lacerated internally, the lips badly cut, all the tips of her fingers were bleeding and ulcerated, her right wrist bore cuts from being struck with a leather strap, and her left hand and arm bore signs of old injuries. Her employers, William Rose, his wife Hannah and daughter Elizabeth, were all arrested and locked up, charged with cruelty. The unfortunate Sarah Ann was fed soup and then sent off to the workhouse. Rough justice indeed!

8 JANUARY   **1844**   William Deakers (aged 29) was sentenced by a Nottingham court to seven years' transportation to the Australian colony after being found guilty of bigamy. He had married a woman named Mary Rose at Radford on 27 December while still married to his first wife Sarah Deakers.

9 JANUARY   **1810**   **An Attempt at Highway Robbery** Mr Hoe, tailor of Bunny near Nottingham, was walking towards the city the previous evening when a man stepped out of the darkness as he approached Ruddington Hill and shouted out, 'Halt and deliver up your money.' Mr Hoe refused, at which point the highwayman drew a sword from under his coat and attacked him. Unfortunately for the robber he had not expected to find his intended victim expert in the use of arms. With only a walking stick for defence, Mr Hoe parried the initial sword thrust, pushed the attacker slowly backwards displaying an expert fencing technique, and eventually divested the robber of his weapon before pushing him backwards into a deep ditch. At that point a second highwayman stepped out from the surrounding undergrowth and, in an attempt to prevent Mr Hoe doing further damage to his partner, stabbed him in the chest after a fierce struggle. But that

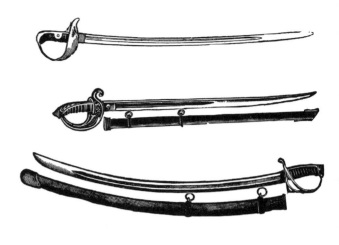

The type of sword likely to have been used in the attack upon Mr Hoe.

evening God was on Mr Hoe's side and the blade, though penetrating all the layers of his clothing, did not succeed in puncturing the flesh, stopped by the pages of his music book, which he had stuffed into an inside pocket earlier that night. Both highwaymen at that point realised the futility of their cause and escaped into the night.

1806 Job Brough, a local Newark councillor (aged 48), was thrown from his horse as he rode to join the hounds on the Great North Road. He died ten days later from a fractured skull while being nursed at his mother's house.

10 JANUARY

1776 The strange funeral of Hannah Waterill took place at St Mary's Church, Nottingham. A very religious woman, Hannah had always attended

11 JANUARY

St Mary's Church, Nottingham, where in the eighteenth century three cemeteries stood close by and where a number of those condemned were buried after their executions.

church on Saturdays dressed in her very best clothes, but on Sundays had always done the opposite wearing her poorest everyday wear, regardless of the rest of the congregation. She had expressed a wish that after her death no man was to be allowed to touch her coffin at her funeral, and that seven bells must peal to register each day of the week.

12 JANUARY 1828 John Dethick (aged 40), a well-known forger, was sentenced to death at Nottingham for 'uttering a forged cheque', worth £10 7s 6d, with intent to defraud city gentleman Frederick Hepworth.

13 JANUARY **1820 A Case of Highway Robbery at Chilwell** Thomas Pearson was held upon the Nottingham road as he drove his gig to Chilwell. Three men stepped out to block his path, one of them holding a pistol, and demanded he hand over all his money. Claiming he had none, Thomas then proceeded to strike out at the armed man using his whip stock. In the fight that ensued he was dragged to the ground, severely beaten, robbed of his watch, pocketbook and £19 in bank notes, and then left for dead. Unfortunately for the man with the pistol, Thomas survived and was able to identify his attacker; he was arrested within days and imprisoned. At his trial three months later Thomas Wilcox pleaded not guilty. His defence argued that it had been too dark for his face to be clearly seen but Thomas Pearson told the court that the moonlight had been clear enough to see by. The jury accepted this statement and Wilcox was duly executed.

14 JANUARY 1814 After thirteen weeks of severe frost across Nottinghamshire temperatures fell to a low of −17°C and the River Trent froze over. People flocked to see the spectacle and the more adventurous skated on the ice as huge bonfires were lit on river banks. It was officially the worst winter since 1795.

15 JANUARY 1824 John Gilbert (aged 21) and John Smith (19) were sentenced to seven years' transportation after being found guilty of stealing 'twelve pairs of pattens valued at 12s' from a Nottingham trader.

16 JANUARY 1884 An inquest was held at the Markham Moor Inn, Tuxford, near Retford, into the discovery of a woman's body found on the Retford road. The woman had been identified as Hannah Lyon. No marks of violence or robbery had been found and according to coroner John Housley there was nothing to indicate the manner or reason of her death. After a short hearing he returned a straightforward, if unsatisfactory, verdict of 'found dead on the highway'.

17 JANUARY 1772 An inquest held at Nottingham's Guildhall declared that Thomas Smith had committed suicide. His body, which had been discovered with its throat slashed open, was ordered to be interred without a coffin and with no Christian rites alongside the highway on the Derby road, in an area known locally as the sand hills.

1892   The *Newark Advertiser* reported the case of policeman Charles Curl,
who appeared before the bench at Newark's petty sessions charged with
having assaulted Sarah Ann Hemshall. Two weeks earlier this young woman,
a domestic servant at a local farm, had been sent out at around eight p.m. to
buy bread. According to her testimony, the policeman had shone his light
on her as she stood knocking on the door of Mr Ricketts, publican and baker.
He asked her what she was about and then grabbed hold of her, forcing her
across the road and into a small alleyway. There she claimed he had put an
arm around her neck and behaved in an indecent manner. She had screamed,
which forced him to release her, and she then ran back to the farmhouse at
Hockerton. Her employer, Mrs Rickett, had then alerted the police. Constable
Curl denied any impropriety and in court no witness could be found who had
heard Sarah's screams. Despite the lack of evidence her story was believed and
Curl was sent to prison for two months' hard labour.

1826   Crowds flocked to St Mary's Church, Nottingham when it became
known that 'resurrection men' had been raiding the graveyard since the
previous November, stealing bodies from graves and selling them on to
unscrupulous medical establishments. The previous day a man named Smith
had taken a large wicker hamper to Pickford's yard in Leen Side, asking for
it to be sent to London on the next coach. Unfortunately for Smith the clerk
who noted down the details for despatch was suspicious about the package
and questioned its owner at length about its origin and content. Smith became
agitated and eventually, after refusing to reveal what was inside the hamper,
left the warehouse on the excuse of needing to consult with his partner. The
clerk ordered one of the Pickford porters, a man named Joseph Arnold, to
follow Smith and report where he went. Arnold returned a short time later to
say that he had seen Smith and another man in a yard close by putting a horse
to a cart and in his opinion making preparations to ride off. Now extremely
suspicious, the clerk, urging Arnold to show him the yard, ran off to attempt
to prevent the escape. Between the two of them they managed to stop the cart
from leaving the yard but after a fight both Smith and the cart driver, a man
named Giles, succeeded in escaping. The local constable was called out and
accompanied the clerk and Arnold back to Leen Side. Inside the basket they
found two bodies. One was that of an old woman, her mouth stuffed with
straw, the other was of a small boy. Both had been dead at least a week. The
woman was later named as Dorothy Townsend, who had died the previous
Sunday, while the boy was identified by his mother who told the authorities
she had only buried him three days earlier. News rapidly spread, and crowds
of people equipped with shovels gathered. Frantically they set about digging
up the graves of their recently buried family to make certain the bodies had
been undisturbed. In many cases their suspicions were well founded and
within hours it was confirmed that the grave-robbers had stolen a total of
thirty bodies. Every grave robbed had been dug within the last four weeks and
the bodies taken had included children. Parsimonious to the last, the families
nevertheless carried away the empty coffins to be used again in the future.

20 JANUARY   **1720**   The *Nottingham Weekly Courant* reported that a great flood had swept through Nottingham as the snow which had been accumulating since Christmas began to thaw. Water levels in the River Trent rose so high it burst its banks rendering all roads into the town impassable; the bridge spanning the river was severely damaged. No post had arrived in Nottingham since 17 January. Countless people had drowned in the flood and the body of one unnamed woman found floating in a field to the east of the city had been partially devoured by crows.

21 JANUARY   **1892**   Herbert Hardy, a painter of Wood Street, Newark, appeared before Newark magistrates charged with cruelty towards three of his children. A cruel, vengeful and vindictive man, he had beaten his children ever since his wife's death six years earlier. Unfortunately for 12-year-old Annie, the eldest of the trio, she had been on the receiving end of the majority of those beatings. Examined a week earlier by local doctor Mr Hallowes, she was found to have sustained significant bruising along both arms, shoulders and much of her back, with one extremely large bruise beneath her left shoulder blade, which the doctor believed had been caused by a blunt instrument. He called in the police. Two days later Inspector Mason examined Annie and found that, apart from the bruising described by the doctor, she had also sustained a bad cut to her left hand and a black eye, both inflicted since the doctor's visit. Under questioning Annie told Mason that her father had beaten her and her two younger sisters with a stick and a coal hammer. Hardy denied systematic abuse and claimed that he had 'thrashed' his children on occasion but never beaten them. But the doctor told the court that the injuries on Annie's back were consistent with having been struck by the flat head of a hammer and that it was quite possible that such a hammer had been used to break up coal. The magistrates refused to accept any plea in mitigation and Hardy was sent to prison for a derisory two months' hard labour, although he was warned that if he re-offended after his release he would be sent back for two years.

22 JANUARY   **1825**   John Handley (aged 22) was found guilty of stealing 4 geese and 5 ducks from a Nottingham farmer, and was sentenced to be transported to Australia for seven years.

23 JANUARY   **1892**   Police made a shocking discovery after forcing their way into a milliner's shop on Arkwright Street, Nottingham. Neighbour Ann Smith had reported to police at St John's police station that Margaret Castings (aged 32), who owned the millinery and haberdashery shop, had not opened the shop for over a week and neither she nor her children had been seen. Police Sergeant Asher was immediately sent to investigate. After forcing his way in through the cellar he discovered the bodies of two young children, later identified as 11-year-old Margaret and 8-year-old Ernest, lying on the kitchen floor. Both had been savagely beaten about the head. Upstairs in a bedroom he found the partially clothed body of the children's mother lying across a bed. Her throat had been cut and the razor used lay on a dressing table, in front

of a blood-spattered mirror. According to the sergeant's report, a pool of dried blood had spread across the carpet in front of this dressing table, which indicated that she had committed suicide while staring at her reflection, before falling back onto the bed. All the doors and windows to the shop and house adjoining had been secured from the inside. Exactly why Margaret Castings had chosen to murder her family in such a brutal manner before taking her own life was never explained.

A Victorian cut-throat razor.

1892 Nottinghamshire was bracing itself for the arrival of the influenza epidemic that was sweeping across Europe and had already affected much of England. Newspapers reported that Prince Henry of Prussia was the latest prominent figure to succumb to the disease, and that doctors in Peterborough and Grantham had to call in assistance from wherever they could, simply to cope with the vast numbers of ailing patients.

24 JANUARY

1874 After the results of the General Election were announced a mob began to riot through the streets of Nottingham, smashing shop windows and street lights across the city. They ended up on Trent Bridge, where they were finally dispersed by the army.

25 JANUARY

1344 According to parish records Margery Doubleseay (often called Doubleday), a washerwoman of Nottingham, took her job extremely seriously. Upon her death she decreed that her 'modest estate', said to exceed £100, be given to the church. The money was to be used to pay for the ringing of a church bell, inscribed:

26 JANUARY

> Aue Maria of you charitie
> For to pray for the sole of
> Magere Dubbyseay.

This bell was to be rung at 6 a.m. to rouse the washerwomen of Nottingham to their labours. Whether it was well received by them is not recorded!

1884 After a long chase through the woodland around Retford, Joe Smith, alias John Smith, was finally captured and brought to the town lock-up. An itinerant beggar, he had been for some time living in a makeshift hovel on the outskirts of Retford and was suspected of a number of burglaries. When searched, the desperate shelter revealed a number of items that had been stolen earlier in the day from the lonely farmhouse of local man William Chapman, who lived with his sister Mary Jane. She it was who discovered

27 JANUARY

the robbery and subsequently identified the items taken from the farmhouse. Smith was sent to Nottingham to stand trial.

28 JANUARY 1802 Governor Wall of Goree in Africa, alias George Armstrong, surgeon of Bingham, Nottingham, was executed on this day at 8 a.m. He had been found guilty of causing the death of a soldier, also named Armstrong, some twenty years earlier in 1782 while in Africa. This unfortunate soldier had been tied to a gun and whipped 800 times by black slaves. His offence? He had demanded of the Governor a sum of back-pay, which he insisted the army owed him. Wall had taken umbrage at the soldier's attitude and after declaring the claim unjustified had ordered the severe punishment in order to uphold his own authority. Apprehended under a warrant issued by the Privy Council in 1784 as he set foot back on British soil, he managed to escape and went to France. There he stayed for eighteen years and would never have been brought to justice had he not written a letter to Lord Pelham in London. Tired of living as a fugitive from the law he had requested in this letter that he be allowed to return to England. Believing that all those who had witnessed the event of 1782 were dead, thus removing any possibility of a trial, he could see no reason for his continued exile. Granted permission to return, he was promptly arrested a second time as his ship docked. Brought to trial, he was told by the judge, Mr Justice Rooke, 'You have occasioned the death of a fellow creature by an unprecedented severity of punishment and by employing an instrument of a novel nature and calculated to produce that terrible and inhuman effect. This you did under the influence of a wicked and inhuman spirit, at a time when no mutiny existed. . . .' On the scaffold before a huge and extremely hostile crowd, he declared as he stepped into eternity that his sins were 'greater in number than the hairs on my head'.

29 JANUARY 1835 On this day Elizabeth Cliff was burnt to death in an accidental fire at her home in Burton Joyce. The church records detailed the epitaph to be placed on her headstone:

> This monumental stone records the name
> Of her who perished in the night by flame
> Sudden and awful, for her hoary head;
> She was brought here to sleep amongst the dead.
> Her loving husband strove to damp the flame
> Till he was nearly sacrificed the same.
> Her sleeping dust, tho' by thee rudely trod,
> Proclaims aloud, prepare to meet thy god.

30 JANUARY 1784 In court at Retford, Ann Castledine stood accused of the murder of her newborn baby. Known by her neighbours to have been heavily pregnant, she had suddenly been observed 'being much alter'd in the size and shape of her belly', but with nothing to show for the sudden change. They alerted the churchwarden and he in turn had forced her arrest. Pleading innocence,

A genuine Account of a moſt Barbarous Cruel and Unnatural
MURDER,

Committed by ANN CASTLEDINE, on the Body of her own Infant, the latter end of January laſt, 1784, at Lownd, near Retford, in the County of NOTTINGHAM, for which ſhe is now a Priſoner in the County Gaol.

THE brutal Woman, who is the ſubjeЄt of this Paper, lived at a Village called Lownd, in the North Clay, a few miles from Retford. Two years ſince, ſhe was tried at Nottingham Affize, on an indiЄtment for murdering her female baſtard child; and tho' there was every reaſon to believe ſhe had been guilty of ſo foul a crime, yet by the lenity of the Judge, and a merciful Jury, ſhe was then acquitted, tho' with a pathetic charge from the Judge, to be very careful of her future conduЄt.

But notwithſtanding the narrow eſcape ſhe then had from a violent death; notwithſtanding the advice of her Judge, and the joy of her friends, on the occaſion, we find ſhe became more abandoned, loſt all ſenſe of honor, or ſhame, and led the life (tho' in a country village) of a common proſtitute. The conſequence of which has been, that ſhe was again pregnant.

Strange as it may appear, this Anne Caſtledine, tho' ſhe had led a vicious a life, tho' ſhe had ſo recently eſcaped the hands of the executioners, yet ſhe would noſ confeſs that ſhe was with child, tho' within two months of her delivery, and even abuſed thoſe who kindly offered their aſſiſtance.

On Friday the 30th of January laſt, one of her neighbours, obſerved that ſhe was much alter'd in the ſize and ſhape of her belly; that ſhe look'd very pale and thin: She then communicated her ſuſpicions to another neighbour. It was then agreed to call a kind of female oouncil, who ſoon met; and after half an hour's conſultation, they agreed to ſend for the churchwarden and overſeer of the poor of the pariſh; and they all concurred in opinion, that Anne Caſtledine, had certainly been with child, and that ſhe appeared to have by ſome means or other, loſt her late burthen.

It was then agreed that two of the women, ſhould watch her, narrowly, and try to make a further diſcovery; but this artful woman, put on ſo chearful a countenance, and went about her buſineſs, with ſuch alacrity, that they began to hope they had miſtaken the caſe. But the overſeer not ſatisfied, ſaid the beſt method would be to obtain a warrant from a Juſtice of Peace, on ſuſpicion of her having murdered her child. The officers applied to Mr. Maſon, one of the

Juſtices of the Peace, at Retford. That gentleman iſſued his warrant for apprehending her.

The conſtable of Lownd, and the overſeer, the ſame day made her their priſoner; but ſhe did not ſeem at all alarmed, and denied her having of late been with child; but not ſatisfied with her proteſtations; they ſent for a midwife, and told Caſtledine if the midwife ſhould be of opinion, their ſuſpicions had not been well founded, ſhe ſhould then be at full liberty. To this ſhe conſented; and the midwife with the aſſiſtance of a worthy matron, of the pariſh, retired to a chamber, and in half an hour returned, with their opinion, that ſhe had certainly been with child, and had lately been delivered; but whether of a living or dead child, it was not in their judgement to determine.

The priſoner, Anne Caſtledine, finding it in vain to deny any longer, the crime laid to her charge; made a voluntary confeſſion, that ſhe had really been with Child; that it came alive into the world, and lived ſome hours, and having then time and opportunity (being alone) ſhe had ſtrangled the infant with her hands.----It was ſome time before ſhe could be prevailed on to ſay what was become of the infant, bnt at laſt ſhe own'd ſhe had put it in the inſide of a chaff bed, where the poor Babe was ſoon found, by the Woman, with many marks of violence on it's Head and Neck.

Saturday laſt the Coroners Inqueſt ſat on the Body of ihe murdered infant, at Lownd, and after viewing the body and examining the midwife, and examining the other witneſſes, they return'd a verdiЄt of WILFUL MURDER, committed by Ann Caſtledine on her own Baſtard Child.

On Sunday the 1ſt of this month, February the ſaid Ann Caſtledine was committed by virtue of a warrant ſigned by Mr. Maſon one of his Majeſtys Juſtices of the Peace for this County, to take her trial for the above mutder at the next Lent Affize for the County of Nottingham.

We are inform'd the priſoner ſeems quite reſigned to her fate, and we hope ſhe will make good uſe of the ſhort time ſhe has to live in this world, by true repentance, and a due preparation for eternity.

Broadsheet from 1784 detailing the trial of and murder committed by Ann Castledine. (Nottingham Local Studies Library)

Ann told the Retford court that the neighbours had been wrong and that she had not been pregnant, and she insisted she had not committed any murder. But the court knew her of old. All too aware that she had been acquitted of exactly the same type of killing two years earlier, the judge was not inclined to accept her story a second time without medical corroboration. He instructed that she be examined by a midwife. This proved to be her undoing. Ann was forced to change her story and admitted to having strangled the newborn baby. The little body was discovered hidden behind her own bed at her home. Sent to trial in Nottingham in March the same year she was found guilty and sentenced to death. After execution her body was given up for dissection to Derby doctor Mr Fox. As it lay on his dissecting table a mysterious gentleman arrived on horseback. Without identifying himself he entered the doctor's house, took up Ann's bloody heart, kissed it, squeezed some blood on to his handkerchief and then remounted his horse and rode away.

31 JANUARY **1884** A report in the *Newark Advertiser* detailed the discovery of the body of 48-year-old William Hutchinson, a Bingham man, in the Nottingham Canal. At the inquest, held at the London Road mortuary in Nottingham, Dr Taylor, who had carried out the post-mortem, told the court that though the man had clearly drowned he had received a severe blow to the head before entering the water. This blow had fractured Hutchinson's skull and would almost certainly have rendered him incapable of climbing out of the canal once he had either fallen or been pushed in. Other witness evidence told the court that Hutchinson had been drinking in the Chesterfield Arms, Bingham, before boarding a train to Nottingham but he had not been seriously intoxicated. Those who knew him, including his wife Fanny, told the coroner that he had shown no signs of depression, and no notable suicidal tendencies. But neither had there been any signs of robbery. Nothing had been stolen from him and no one had seen any fight. The coroner returned a verdict of 'found drowned'.

FEBRUARY

A seventeenth-century woodcut of a public execution.

Trials and Execution,

Of George Beck, aged 20, **George Hearson, aged 22,**

and John **Armstrong, aged 26,**

Who suffered Death, at the New Drop, on the County Hall Steps, on Wednesday, February 1, 1832, for riotously assembling and Burning the Silk Mill, at Beeston, the property of Mr. William Lowe.

In consequence of the Riots which took place at Nottingham, Colwick, and Beeston, on the 9th, 10th, and 11th of October last, many persons were taken into custody. His Majesty, therefore, with the advice of his Ministers, issued a Special Commission for the trial of the Prisoners, which Commission was opened in due form on the 6th of January.

On Friday, Jan. 6, George Beck, was first put on his trial, charged with setting fire to the silk mill at Beeston in this County, the property of Mr. W. Lowe, and to the dwelling house of George Turton the elder, and George Turton the younger.

William Turton, examined by Mr. Gurney—In the month of October last, I was employed at Beeston mill; on Tuesday the 11th, a mob came there between twelve and one, from the direction of Nottingham, they were between two and three thousand in number; they came along the road, at first two or three deep; there were afterwards about forty in the front rank; there was a person who carried a flag, it was a pole with a riband at the end; Geo. Beck, the prisoner at the bar, was the man; when they came opposite the mill, Beck said, "This is the place," and then the mob immediately threw stones at the mill windows. He then marched a few yards further, till they came opposite to the mill doors, he then said, "Halt, front, fall round, and do your duty;" the front rank marched to the doors of the mill; as soon as they reached the door, some with pump handles, some with palisading, and some with hammers, and every article useful to destroy properly, broke through the doors: somebody crept through the hole and hammered at the lock to break it; the doors were thrown open, and the mob all crowded into the yard, Geo. Beck, the flagman, along with them; then I went away to the workshop, to watch what was going on, when there, I observed persons from the inside of the mill breaking the windows, and silk, soap, and candles, were thrown out; another part of the mob was breaking the machinery, and others setting fire to the place. The mill was burnt down, and every thing consumed.

The Learned Judge occupied more than an hour in recapitulating the evidence, which he did with great exactness; the Jury after consulting together, expressed a wish to retire. After ten minutes, the Jury returned a verdict of Guilty, with a recommendation to mercy, on account of his character, and the evidence of Dodsley, who went part of the way with the rioters.

On Saturday, George Hearson, aged 22, Thomas Shelton, aged 38, and John Armstrong, aged 26, were placed at the bar, and charged with the burning of Beeston mill, on the same indictment as those of Beck.

Wm. Turton then declared the evidence similar to that on the trial of Beck. The case being gone through, the prisoners were called upon for their defence.

George Hearson said, I have witnesses to show where I was when the accident happened. I got up about half-past nine, and had my breakfast; my wife and I went out to look at the ruins of the Castle; in the Market-place we met Methringham and his wife, and afterwards Wilkinson and his wife; and somewhere about the Castle I met William Daykin; we remained till twelve o'clock, when we heard the mob was gone to Beeston, to set fire to the mill, we agreed to go; we went through Lenton, and up a narrow lane, which brought us into Beeston turnpike; when we got there, the biggest part of the mob was returned, and the mill was all in flames, and a part of the roof fallen in; we returned, and got back about two o'clock. I am as innocent as the child unborn.

John Armstrong said—I was very fresh on Tuesday, and was led away by the mob. I hope you will have mercy upon me, my years are but young.

Thomas Shelton said—All I have to say I have already told the magistrates. I have lived in Beeston many years and no one can say any thing against my character. The bar of iron that they said that I carried, It was a piece of flat iron, about an inch broad, and two foot long; that I took out of a man's hand just before we got to Beeston. I told the Magistrates I never was in the mill.

Mr. Justice Gazelee summed up the evidence with great minuteness, and the jury, after deliberating for about three minutes, returned a verdict of Guilty against all the three prisoners.

On the verdict being given, Hearson seemed a good deal surprised.

On Saturday Jan. 14, Mr. Justice Littledale proceeded to pass sentence; he addressed Beck, Hearson, Armstrong, and Shelton, telling them that they had been convicted of setting fire to Beeston mill, and Charles Berkins of setting fire to Colwick Hall; that the wisdom of the legislature and the security of the country called for capital punishment on persons who violated the law. He then went into a history of the riots, showed that advantage had been taken of a time of excitement, by a number of wicked and designing men to perpetrate outrages unconnected with the object of the meeting which had assembled in the Market-place. He said that the five whom he was addressing had been so considered, and that they intended to recommend the other four to mercy. His Lordship said to Beck, that he was active in carrying the colours, and baiting the mob; to Hearson, that he carried a bottle of combustible matter, and had been active in the work of destruction; to Armstrong, that he had been active in the work of demolition, and had set fire to a window blind; to Shelton, that he had been concerned in breaking machinery, and setting fire to it; to Berkins, that he had pulled off his shirt, set fire to it, and thrown it under the bed at Colwick. He entreated them to make their peace with God, and endeavour to obtain his favour in the world to come. He concluded by passing the awful sentence of the law in the usual terms.

During the time that the formal and concluding part of the sentence was pronounced, that they should be hanged, the grief of all appeared to be subdued by the hopelessness of their situation; Berkin's countenance became fixed, and as the others turned away to leave the bar of their earthly judge, he sunk to the ground in a fit, and was carried away.

Great interest has been made by the Inhabitants of Nottingham and its Vicinity, to save the lives of these individuals. On Tuesday, Jan. 24th inst. a Petition was sent to the King, signed by 24,000 persons; and on Sunday last, another Petition was also forwarded to the House of Commons in their behalf, and yesterday morning a King's Messenger arrived with a RESPITE for SHELTON and BERKINS.

The unhappy men since their condemnation, upon the whole, have behaved with becoming propriety, each of them reading the scriptures, and praying at intervals; they have been attended by the Rev. Dr. Wood, Chaplain to the Jail, the Rev. Mr. Rolleston, of Beeston, and several ministers in the Wesleyan Connexion have visited them, they have endeavored to convince them of their awful situation, and exhort them to repentance. but in some of these unhappy men, there does not appear that contrition, or change of mind that could be wished of persons in such circumstances. Armstrong, in particular, seemed less concerned respecting his future state, to some questions put to him he replied "that a rough stone took a deal of polishing." Hearson was penitent at times, but wavering in his mind. Beck seemed to await his awful exit, with resignation. The conduct of Shelton and Berkins was very becoming their awful situation up to the time when the Respite arrived.

On Monday, the heart-rending scene of bidding farewell to their relatives and friends, took place, it was a scene more to be felt than described, the thought of bidding an eternal adieu to all worldly affections, is sufficient to subdue the stoutest heart, all were bathed in tears, and the unhappy men seemed truly to feel the state of their deplorable situation.

Preparations for the Execution was began yesterday in front of the County Hall, where a temporary drop was erected.

This morning, all being in readiness for the melancholy spectacle, and the Sheriff having arrived with his assistants, the wretched men were brought out the ropes being properly adjusted, the caps being drawn over their faces, the signal was then given, the drop fell, and they were launched into Eternity.

Hearson and Armstrong are natives of Nottingham, and Beck of Wollaton, near Nottingham. Hearson has left a wife and one child, the other two were not married.

T. KIRK, PRINTER, NOTTINGHAM

Broadsheet of the triple execution of Beck, Hearson and Armstrong, detailing their crime. (Nottingham Local Studies Library)

1832 A triple drop at Nottingham Three men, George Beck (aged 20), George Hearson (22) and John Armstrong (26), were all executed together in front of Nottingham's County Hall. On 4 January Armstrong had been found guilty of causing the Beeston riot and the destruction of Lowe's silk mill. The other two had been arrested later the same month and charged with involvement in the same crime. Unfortunately for Beck and Hearson, though, their convictions had been made on spurious identification evidence. No one at their trial had given irrefutable evidence to establish guilt and by the time they climbed on to the scaffold to join Armstrong some 24,000 people had signed petitions for their release and well over that number swelled the crowds which gathered to watch the executions. So nervous were the Nottingham officials that they called out the 15th Hussars, The Queens Bays, the 18th Foot and a significant body of special constables to block off High Pavement and prevent any outbreak of unrest. A poem relating the injustice of the verdicts was widely circulated:

> Hark! The Trumps are mournful sounding,
> Wafting souls to realms above,
> Where there's naught but bliss abounding,
> Glorying too for Jesu love.
>
> The reckless fate of these poor creatures,
> Fills the town with sad dismay,
> For Nottingham, with its bright features,
> Could not check that dreadful day.
>
> To see the prime of youth now wither,
> 'Midst relations, friends so dear,
> It makes one's blood almost to shiver,
> Who could stop the burning tear?
>
> Hearson, Beck and Armstrong boldly,
> Met their fates beneath the tree;
> Villains swore against them coldly,
> And their doom we all shall see.

1772 On this day Nottingham's local press reported details of a great snowstorm that had raged across the city throughout the night and into the early hours of the day. The severest storm in living memory, it claimed the lives of numerous people, including Mrs Ann Webster of Calverton, who had left Nottingham in the late afternoon just as the snow began to fall, intending to ride home. Caught in the teeth of the blizzard, her body was found shortly after dawn, still astride her horse and her frozen hands still clutching the reins. Both horse and rider were quite dead. A similar fate befell butler Thomas Rhodes and his good friend John Curtis. Attempting to drive their carriage into the city they were halted at Newstead by a soldier in great distress. Thomas, fearing the man

Gateway to
Nottingham prison.

would die without assistance, kindly unhitched one of his horses and sent the soldier off toward Mansfield. It saved his life, but it was the undoing of the two travelling companions. They were both found dead several hours later, along with their remaining horses which had refused to move as the weather worsened.

1865 Charles Towle was hauled up before magistrates in Nottingham and charged with the offence of throwing snowballs. Hannah Dakin claimed he had made an unprovoked attack on her and thrown snowballs at her head in a street in Stapleford. The snowballs, she claimed, had hurt her when they struck and had knocked her to the floor. Magistrates took a sympathetic view and poor old Charles was fined 20s and told to refrain from such actions in the future.

3 February

1775 Footpads attacked and robbed James Broome of 23s 9d at Basford, Nottingham, but Broome was a resourceful man and not easily separated from his wealth. Recognising one of his attackers as James Porter, a man he had been drinking beer with only hours earlier, he resolved to track him down. Believing Porter to be less than intelligent and probably in need of another drink, he felt it unlikely that he would have strayed far from the warmth of the pub's fireside. Thus he retraced his steps. He found Porter, as he had expected, propping up the bar and merrily spending some of the silver shillings he had just stolen. In the fight that ensued Broome won the day and a badly beaten James Porter gave up what remained of his share of the robbery. The others involved unfortunately escaped.

4 February

1885 It was reported in the *Colonial Gazette* that Nottingham woman Annie Pagel, shipwrecked off the coast of North New Guinea, had been captured by a warlike tribe of Hermit islanders and, along with other members of the ship's crew, eaten at a cannibal banquet. A native of an adjoining island, who had also been captured but had escaped, is said to have confirmed the story. A search of the area by a German vessel apparently recovered a white chemise bearing the embroidered initials A.P.

5 February

1909 The *Nottingham Daily Express* reported the mysterious death of 46-year-old Annie Tantum at Hyson Green, Nottingham. She had been found at the bottom of a flight of stairs alight from head to foot. Nothing else in the downstairs rooms showed any kind of fire damage. A police search of the upper rooms revealed that in Annie's bedroom the dressing table had been knocked over, three beer bottles had been smashed and lay scattered across the floor, a lamp had been broken and a small patch of curtain showed some fire damage. However, there was nothing to indicate how or where the fire had started. According to Dr Alloway, the house surgeon at Nottingham General Hospital, she had suffered severe burns across every part of her body and died within six hours of being admitted. Coroner Mr Rothera, declared the case to be a complete mystery and the jury agreed in a verdict of 'Died from burns, but there was no evidence to show how her clothing became ignited'.

6 February

7 February **1773** The remains of William Rice, the 'Nottingham giant', were buried a St Anne's Church, Sutton Bonnington, on this day. The coffin, made of stron oak, was 8ft 4in long, and the grave measured 9ft in length and 7ft deep. I took eight stout men to carry the coffin into the church, followed by eigh maids who bore the pall. The church was packed with over 500 mourners.

8 February **1801** Ralph Kinder (aged 44) was condemned to death after being foun guilty of stealing and killing a wedder sheep (castrated male) from a field ir Basford and then trying to sell the meat.

9 February **1795** After forty-seven days of severe frost, during which the River Tren had frozen over as far as Gainsborough, a thaw began that caused the rive to burst its banks. The fast-moving water swept away fence-posts, rails, trees flocks of sheep and numerous cattle. Most of the people living in Narrov Marsh, Nottingham, were trapped in their homes by the floodwater. The cana system was destroyed and all the livestock housed at West Bridgford, Wilforc and Lenton were completely wiped out.

10 February **1823** The *Nottingham Date Book* (a history of Nottingham from AD 850 tc 1884 by Mr J.F. Sutton) includes a report of a burglary. George Lackenby (aged 21) was arrested shortly after stealing three pairs of shoes and a boo from the Nottingham home of Charles Shaw. Just what he hoped to do witl one boot was never made clear, but for Lackenby it was to be the last burglar he would ever commit. Found guilty at his trial, he was originally sentencec to death but this was later commuted to transportation for life.

11 February **1902** **A Strange Death at Bingham** An inquest held at the Wheat Sheaf Inn Bingham, heard how the body of gardener Edward Coy had been found lying in the middle of the Bingham to Langar road a few days earlier at a little after 10 a.m. He had sustained head injuries and his bicycle was parked by the roadside resting on the hedgerow. A number of witnesses told the court they had met him during the course of the morning, some having held brie conversations with him, and his body had been found within minutes of the last of these short meetings. No other person was seen either on the road o crossing the fields. Coroner Frederick Footitt decided that he had probably fallen from his bicycle and sustained the injuries that killed him, but of course there could be no certainty.

12 February **1847** **Death of Darker, the Recluse** Known as Tommy to those that knew him Darker lived a hermit-like existence in a house at Broadmarsh, Nottingham Born to a wealthy family, he had remained a bachelor throughout his life and consistently shunned all modern amenities. So miserly had he become in olc age that he only spent 2s a week on food, performed all his household dutie; between 11 p.m. and midnight, regarded fire as a luxury he rarely indulgec in, preferring to stay in bed if it were cold, dressed like a beggar and refusec to allow anyone into his house. Committed to an asylum a year earlier, he

…ad died in a state of total madness after refusing to allow anyone to enter
…his property to cap a dangerous well. After the funeral it was discovered that
…onsiderable quantities of gold and valuable securities were stored in a back
…oom in the house he had so fiercely guarded.

1909 A case of Proverbs in Justice The *Nottingham Daily Express* reported the   13 FEBRUARY
…ase of Mary Saunders of Platt Street, Nottingham, who appeared in court
…ith a summons against her husband for desertion for a fourth time and
was told by the judge 'Sufficient unto the day is the evil
thereof'. Turning to the representing solicitor he then
advised them 'to pour oil on troubled waters', and to
the sergeant, who had stood in the witness box and
called the troubled couple 'vinegary', he pointed
out that 'the milk of human kindness filtered
downwards'. But, answered the sergeant, 'Even
the worm will turn', and in the case of the put-
upon husband 'the turn has come' and he 'will not
have her back'. 'Then he should not,' replied the
magistrate, and a bemused Mary Saunders left the
court with her summons dismissed.

1892 An inquest held at the Shireoaks Hotel near   14 FEBRUARY
Worksop heard how 24-year-old David Spivey had
thrown himself in front of the 10 a.m. Sheffield train
because the woman he loved had jilted him. Ellsa
Wilcon, the woman in question, had never been
in love with Spivey and when the two had met in
Carolgate, Retford, a week earlier she had told
him that their brief relationship was at an end,
she had met someone else and did not wish to
see him again. She wrote him a letter a few days
later explaining in a little more detail just why
they had to part. Spivey expressed a great deal of
anger at Ellsa's decision and told friends he was going to cut his own
…hroat, even showing them the razor he had bought to do the job with. No
…ne believed him capable of such an act. At some point after the conversation
…e obviously changed his mind about his chosen method, possibly because
…e could not pluck up the courage to kill himself in such a calculated way.
Instead he walked across to the railway lines close to where he lived and
…tepped in front of the first train to pass. There was no blood at the scene: the
…rain had smashed his body and fractured his skull, killing him instantly.

1884 Mysterious poisoning at Warsop Ten-year-old Hannah Head was found   15 FEBRUARY
…lead by her stepmother shortly after taking a dose of Epsom salts. According
…o George Stein, the Warsop surgeon called to the house, when he examined
…er body the hands were clenched and the lips livid, which he believed were

Carolgate, Retford,
c. 1936.

distinct signs that Hannah had been poisoned. At the inquest held at the
Hare and Hounds Inn, Warsop, he told the coroner that a post-mortem
examination showed her stomach contained a quantity of Epsom Salts and
strychnine. In fact, more than 3 per cent of the stomach contents contained
the poison. Since half a grain of strychnine was sufficient to cause death, and
the 3 per cent represented a minimum of a grain and a half, there was no
doubt as to how the girl had died. According to Hannah's stepmother, some
strychnine had been purchased over a year earlier to rid the house of rats but
all the remaining poison had been destroyed. There was no way, according
to her evidence, that either she or her husband could have administered
any poison to her stepdaughter. Hannah's father in turn confirmed that
he had poured the surplus poison into a nearby stream ten months earlier,
and added that both the poison and the salts had been purchased from Mr
Blore's chemist's shop in Warsop. The implication was that the chemist had
accidentally mixed the two substances together during preparation, thus
contaminating the Epsom salts. This the chemist strongly contested. He
owned two shops, he said, one in Warsop and one in Mansfield Woodhouse,
and only the Mansfield Woodhouse premises contained strychnine stocks.
But, as the coroner pointed out, according to the label on the packet the
salts had been packaged in the Mansfield Woodhouse branch, not at Warsop,
where Elizabeth Head, Hannah's stepmother, had made the purchase.
If neither of the parents had added poison to the mix, then it had to have
happened at the shop. But other people were known to have purchased Epsom
salts there at around the same time, and there had been no other deaths.

The jury returned a verdict of poisoning but with no evidence of how it had happened, and Hannah Head's death remained a mystery.

1909   Frank Bismark of no fixed abode was sent to prison for a week after being arrested on the platform of Nottingham station for attempting to break into a sweet machine in broad daylight.

16 FEBRUARY

1770   Found murdered on this day was Newark pawnbroker Thomas Burrill. Attacked inside his own shop, he had been brutally beaten and left to die on the floor. Three men were quickly arrested, William Hebb, Daniel Hebb and Thomas Moore. Within hours of the arrest William Hebb made a full and frank confession in which he insisted that he alone had committed the killing. The other two, according to his statement, were merely accessories to the fact and could not have known that he had intended to murder the shopkeeper when they had forced a way into his shop. Their trial opened four weeks later and the jury, after listening to Hebb's version of events, decided to take a lenient view. His confession was accepted and his two co-conspirators were acquitted. Accepting the sentence of death which was passed upon him, William Hebb made one final request – that Daniel Hebb, his cousin, be allowed to execute him. The court agreed, but when William stood beneath the noose Daniel lost his nerve and refused to be his hangman. Without further ado William placed the noose around his own neck and jumped off the cart into eternity.

17 FEBRUARY

1825   At his trial in Nottingham William Armstrong (aged 35) was found guilty of stealing 3½yds of woollen cloth from the home of Samuel Daft. The judge declared him a menace to society and sentenced him to death.

18 FEBRUARY

1909   On this day 89-year-old William Roe, of Hyson Green, Nottingham, was discovered in a back bedroom of his house, horrifically burnt after a fire had broken out at his terraced home. The old man had sat down to his evening meal unaware that a blazing fire raged beneath his feet. Alive when firefighters stumbled across his body, he died later in hospital.

19 FEBRUARY

1827   John Wesley (aged 19) and James White were arrested shortly after robbing a Nottingham house of 3 coats, 3 bedsheets, a pair of trousers and various other household items valued at 40s. While in custody they implicated Elizabeth Smith (aged 25), who was to have sold the goods on. At their trial the two men were found guilty and sentenced to death. Elizabeth was slightly more fortunate; she was sentenced to fourteen years' transportation.

20 FEBRUARY

1885   An inquest held at the Midland Hotel, Mansfield, heard how 16-month-old Roseta Pearson had fallen head first into a bucket of boiling water, which her father, unaware that she was behind him, had placed on the kitchen floor. Curiosity had got the better of her and she died some hours later.

21 FEBRUARY

EXTRACT OF A

LETTER,

And a copy of Verses, written by Valentine Marshall, now in Van Dieman's Land, to his Friends in Nottingham

A letter recently received, written by Valentine Marshall, now in Van Dieman's Land, to his friends in Nottingham, states:—"That when I arrived at Hobart Town I was sent about fifty miles up the country, to fill the situation of a shepherd's boy; in this situation I was comparatively happy, my master being a kind and indulgent man. My good conduct in this situation soon gained me the respect of my master, and he kindly endeavoured to obtain a remission of my sentence. I was now sent back to Hobart Town, and became a messenger to the Governor of the jail, which situation I now hold; this change I chiefly attribute to the kindness of General Furguson, who has interceded on my behalf. My labours in my new place are not very great, and were I not absent from all my friends, I could rest contented. The state of the country is not so promising to settlers as it was when I first arrived, owing, I suppose, to the great number of transports and emigrants which almost daily arrive, in hopes of improving their condition, many of whom would be glad to return to England if they could obtain a passage back."

Nottingham, February 18, 1834.

GOOD people give attention, and
  listen to my tale,
The truth of my misfortunes, I will
  quickly reveal;
I being young and foolish, my years
  just turned sixteen,
When Judge Littledale did me transport for being on Colwick Green

It was on the 10th of October, as
  many well do know,
Along with several thousands, I to
  Colwick Hall did go;
There I nothing did but looked on,
  such a sight I ne'er had seen,
Judge Littledale did me transport
  for being on Colwick Green.

The mischief partly over, great damage there was done,
Along with several others I did return straight home;
Where I nothing to my parents said,
  about where I had been,
And so the Judge transported me
  for being on Colwick Green.

There was many apprehended, and
  many run away,
But conscious of my innocence, I
  with my friends did stay;
Till young Freeman of Old Sneinton
  he swore he me had seen,
And so the Judge did me transport
  for being on Colwick Green.

Then I was apprehended and to the
  jail was sent,
Which caused me and my parents,
  my case for to lament;
Till being tried by a Jury, such a
  one that ne'er had been,
And so the Judge did me transport
  for being on Colwick Green.

Our trials being over, nine of us
  were cast,
Which made...

Neither our youth or characters,
  would cause them to relent,
'Twas clear to every one of us, they
  were on example bent.
One painful observation to you I
  wish to make,
The morning we left Nottingham,
  how sore our hearts did ache;
There was neither friend or parent,
  to take their last farewell,
The time of our departure they
  would not to us tell.

But now I'm in Van Dieman's land,
  where happy I could be,
Where it not for my parents, their
  grief I can't relieve;
But I hope the Lord in goodness,
  will blessings on them send,
And such troubles in Old England,
  I hope they soon may end.

Now to the girl that I respect, tho'
  from her forced to part,
The token I last received from her,
  I sealed it to my heart;
An I should it please kind providence
  we should single meet again,
Our troubles shall be buried in a
  connubial chain.

So now to General Furguson one
  toast I wish to give,
He is a kind old gentleman, and I
  wish him long to live,
All for the trouble which he bestow'd
  my case for to amend,
Through his Scotish heart I found a
  goodness to the end.

O may you never forsake him, so
  long as he's inclin'd
Your interests to watch over, for
  he's a noble mind;
And his sound deliberations doth
  mean well in the end,
Though Tories with some violence
  against him may contend.

Now to my friends in Nottingham,
  that to me was so kind,
The favours I received from them,
  I shall ever bear in mind;
And may Reform your hearts make
  glad, for if that before had been,
No Judge would have transported
  me for being on Colwick Green.

A broadsheet account of the trials of Valentine Marshall, dated 18 February 1834, written as letters and verses and then sold by him throughout Nottingham. (Nottingham Local Studies Library)

1909   Two days after the banns were read out announcing his impending marriage, Samuel Marriott, head gardener to a Newark house, walked into an outhouse and shot himself through the head.

1906   The unfortunate story of Edith Martin was told to a Nottingham court. Married for three years, she had been regularly beaten by her husband Martin. Throughout their married life, he had wasted all his money backing horses and when his own money ran out he spent the housekeeping. In the sad and sorry tale she told the court, she detailed numerous occasions when neither of them had eaten because there was no money to buy food and he was refused credit at all the shops around their home. Their own child had been put out to nurse because he refused to have it in the house, and on more than one occasion she herself had been physically ejected from her home. The final straw had come on Boxing Day, when during a fight at her in-laws' house she had sustained two black eyes. The husband, of course, denied each and every accusation – and despite all the evidence to the contrary the judge accepted his denial. Dismissing the case of cruelty, he ordered the couple to reconcile their differences.

22 FEBRUARY

23 FEBRUARY

Above: Parliament Street, Nottingham, *c.* 1900.

24 February

1909 Collier Robert Asman pleaded guilty to having thrown vitriol into his fiancée's face because she refused to kiss him. The woman involved, Janet Kendall, had been severely disfigured around her mouth and eyes. Despite this, she astonished the court by pleading for leniency for Asman. After giving evidence of how Asman had deliberately thrown the liquid into her face because she had pushed him away, she told the Mansfield judge that she still intended to marry him. Incredulous at this admission, the judge asked her why, pointing out that marriage was for better or worse and, of course, for life. Janet Kendall replied that she earnestly believed Asman would not harm her again. After giving vent to his feelings of astonishment, the judge accepted that she genuinely believed Asman's unprovoked attack had not been premeditated and so acceded, to some extent, to her plea. Nevertheless, as he pointed out to Asman, she would be disfigured for life and that, in his estimation, was unforgivable. He sent Asman to prison for eight months, remarking that the sentence would have been considerably greater had his fiancée not made so extraordinary a plea.

25 February

1909 **The Jacksdale Tragedy** James Holden stood in the dock before Mr Justice Channell and pleaded not guilty to murder. A jealous man, he had come to believe that his wife and a neighbour, Willy Barlow, had been meeting in secret and conducting an affair behind his back. When he found the two of them drinking together in the Portland Arms near Mansfield, he believed he had confirmed his own suspicions despite his wife's denials, and the two had their first public falling-out. But Holden, who outwardly appeared to have accepted his wife's version of events, found it impossible to suppress his jealousy and his doubts boiled over six days later. Without forewarning his wife, he called out to Barlow from the front door of his house as he saw the young man pass his kitchen window, inviting him in. The unsuspecting Barlow readily agreed, possibly hoping there was to be a reconciliation between the two men. But Holden was not a forgiving man. Almost as soon as the young man entered the room he found himself accused of adultery. A row followed, in which Barlow denied the accusation and turned to leave. As he did so Holden struck him a single blow to the back of the head with a hatchet he had purposely brought into the house. As Barlow fell to the floor Holden turned toward his terrified wife, who ran screaming from the room. At that point their son David and a lodger named Beardall burst into the kitchen, alerted by all the noise. They attempted to calm Holden down but it was a hopeless task: he was so intent upon murdering his wife that he simply pushed aside the two men as he lunged at her before she could escape through the open door. But she was fortunate: the blow, although serious, was not fatal. Barlow, on the other hand, was less lucky. Police found him unconscious but alive, and he was immediately taken to hospital. Despite two operations to save his life, he died some three months later. In court Holden wept openly as he realised the hopelessness of his case. But here he too was lucky. His defence counsel was successful in reducing the charge from murder to manslaughter, and at the conclusion of the trial, when the jury

eturned the expected guilty verdict, he
was sentenced to seven years'
imprisonment.

88o The funeral
took place on this
day of James
Lawrence, uncle of the
writer D.H. Lawrence, who
was killed after a roof fall at
Brinkley pit. Polly Lawrence,
his unfortunate wife, was
eight months pregnant at the
time, and gave birth to her third
child one month later.

826 Murder most foul! At around
midnight on this day John Webster, a
Nottingham joiner, returned to his home
on Derby Road after a night out in the Sir
John Warren public house. Despite being
somewhat the worse for wear, he expected to
find the back door unlocked and his supper on
the table. The woman he lodged with, however,
had other ideas. As he banged on the door she
leaned her back against it and refused to pull back
the bolts, shouting at him that he must go elsewhere,
it was dark, and she could not be certain he was her
lodger. Accusing her of madness and undeterred by
her protests, he eventually managed to break in.
Incensed by her attempt to keep him outside, he
grabbed her around the waist and threw her out into
the yard. While all this was going on the neighbours
called out the night watchman, Walter Soar, to try
to calm the situation. But Soar had no time for such
subtleties. Storming into the house with the heavy cosh
he always carried, he simply struck out at Webster and
kept on hitting him until the man was dead.

85o On this day staff at Nottingham's general hospital
removed the skeleton that had hung in its lecture room
for thirty-five years. The wire holding the bones
together had begun to decay and it was decided that
the skeleton could no longer be repaired. On its removal
it was discovered that the bones had once belonged to John Hemstock.
Convicted in 1815 of the brutal murder of a Retford youth, Hemstock had

26 FEBRUARY

27 FEBRUARY

28 FEBRUARY

lived on the edge of the law and was eventually executed for beating to death a young man with an iron bar and afterwards cutting his throat for good measure. His body had been cut down and handed over to Nottingham doctors for dissection.

29 FEBRUARY **Old Nottingham Beliefs and Sayings** If an egg that was laid by a brown hen on Ascension Day is placed upon the roof of your house, then fire will never visit nor burn it to the ground.

A skeleton, like the one that would have hung in Nottingham General Hospital.

MARCH

Nottingham castle as it looked at the start of the twentieth century.

1 MARCH **1909** An inquest held into the discovery of a body beside the railway line at Newark identified the dead man as William Brailsford (aged 39). A guest at the George and Dragon Inn, Newark, he had been travelling back and forth to Nottingham throughout the last week of February searching for employment. He had been missing for two days, and when found his body had been completely frozen by a heavy frost, and the head and hands severed by a passing train. Having heard witness evidence to the effect that he had exhibited no outward signs of depression, the coroner decided that it was likely he had been killed accidentally. The landlord of the George and Dragon had told the court that William enjoyed a stroll each day beside the rail tracks. It would appear that the unfortunate man had forgotten about the trains.

2 MARCH **1680** Joshua Longman, a native of Pleasley, near Derby, was ordered to be whipped in Mansfield after being caught begging in the town.

3 MARCH **1895** William Birkett stood in the dock at Nottingham after being arrested for cruelty to a horse. Police Constable Hawke told the court that the horse was found in a distressed condition, being dragged along the Nottingham road by Hawke and his two children who were constantly beating it because it was moving too slowly. Hawke claimed he had not realised the animal was injured but the bench, after hearing veterinary evidence, sentenced him to a fine of 10s plus court costs or a term in prison. It is not recorded which of the two options he chose.

4 MARCH **1894** **Charged with stealing bones** Clementine Brooks and her son William Brooks were brought before Nottingham magistrates after being found in possession of 87lb of animal bones stolen from a Hucknall warehouse and valued at 3s. Both denied the charge but with a house full of old bones they were hardly likely to be able to talk their way out of prison. Constable Evans who had found the bones in a back room of their Hucknall home, had already had them identified by their owner, Charles Hibbert, though exactly how was not recorded by the court. Mother and son were sent to prison for an unspecified period, but probably no more than one month.

5 MARCH **1909** **Mystery of the mutilated woman** In the early hours of the morning Wilford road lock-keeper George Osgaby discovered a woman's leg lodged behind the lock gate beneath the Wilford road canal bridge. A few hours later a complete torso, minus both legs, was found several hundred yards away by local carter Joe Matthews, Seeing what he thought to be a bundle of clothes floating in the canal, he pulled it toward the walled bank, and only then did he realise it was the body of a woman, or at least what was left of her. Minus both legs and internal organs, she had been horrifically mutilated. Police later confirmed that the woman had been around the age of forty, and was only partially clothed in a bodice and white linen underskirt. The only identifiable objects on her person were two gold rings on her left hand. At the inquest held

Opposite: A poster published by Nottingham Town and County in 1812 warning people not to fire off muskets. (Nottingham Local Studies Library)

TOWN AND COUNTY OF THE
Town of Nottingham.

BY Command of the Magiſtrates, *I am directed to give Notice*, that all manner of Perſons are ſtrictly enjoined and prohibited from firing any Muſquets, Piſtols, or other Fire Arms, either by Night or by Day, within the Town of Nottingham or its immediate Neighbourhood, or ſpringing any Rattle, or making any Noiſe of a ſimilar kind, (except in Caſes of Self-Defence,) under Pain of being proceeded againſt with the utmoſt Rigour of the Law. The Magiſtrates are confident, that every Inhabitant of this Town will ſee the Neceſſity of an immediate Stop being put to a Practice, which has a tendency to ſpread unneceſſary Alarm, and diſtract and confound the Attention of thoſe who are ſtatedly employed in the Protection of the Public Peace; and to render uſeleſs thoſe means of Concert and Co-opera-tion, which the Public Service may render proper to be adopted by the Conſtables and Military Patroles, to whoſe Vigilance, the Peace and Security of the Town is, under the Superintendance of the Magiſtrates, continually confided.

By Order,
GEO. COLDHAM,
TOWN CLERK.

Nottingham, January 28th, 1812.

J. Dunn, Printer, Nottingham.

at Leen Side it was decided that some of the injuries could have been made by a passing steamboat but that there was no way of discovering who the woman was or how she had ended up in the canal. A simple verdict of 'found drowned' was returned.

6 MARCH **1737** James Gibbins, a stone mason of Nottingham, was executed after being found guilty of highway robbery on the Nottingham road.

7 MARCH **1825** In May 1821 George Sparrow (aged 24) had stolen a brown horse from East Retford farmer Edward Parker. The horse was valued at around £59, a considerable sum of money, and Sparrow became a wanted man. Two weeks later he returned to the same area and stole a brown mare from the neighbouring farm of John Dawber. Unfortunately for Sparrow, he was spotted selling the horse on at a fair. An attempt was made to arrest him but he escaped and remained a fugitive for six months. Finally arrested in January 1825, he stood trial on this day and was sentenced to death.

8 MARCH **1782** Found guilty of stealing a bill of exchange worth £120 from the Tuxford to Newark mail-coach on 10 November 1781, after successfully drugging the young driver, Cooper Hall was sentenced to death at his Nottingham trial. He was executed three weeks later.

9 MARCH **1649** On this day Nottinghamshire's most prominent landowner, Arthur, Lord Capel, was executed for his loyalty to Charles I and his involvement in the 1648 uprising. Captured at Colchester after the surrender of the castle, he was originally promised safe passage and given quarter for his life. However Parliament reneged on the offer, put him on trial and pronounced him guilty of treason.

10 MARCH **1643** **Penny Loaf Sunday** Hercules Clay and his family lived in the market square in Newark, and remained there throughout the siege of the castle during the English Civil War. During this time he dreamed three times that his house caught fire but each time he awoke before the dream ended. After the third dream he decided to rouse his family from their beds and vacate the house. As they wandered across the square in the dark an explosion behind them set their house alight. So grateful was Hercules for his escape that he bequeathed a sum of money to Newark Corporation to provide annually a commemorative sermon in the church and a penny loaf for every poor person that needed bread on what became known as 'penny loaf Sunday'.

11 MARCH **1811** Nottingham's framework knitters gathered in the city's market square to protest at the introduction into the mills of new machinery that directly threatened their livelihood. The meeting descended into riot and only the arrival of a regiment of soldiers from the nearby barracks prevented the hostile crowd spilling out across the city and wrecking nearby shops and businesses.

The site today of
Hercules Clay's
house in Newark
market square. A
plaque on the wall
gives some detail of
his dream.

12 MARCH   **1830**   John Watson (aged 23), a labourer of Nottingham, was sentenced to death at Nottingham's courthouse for stealing a coat from a house in Basford six months earlier.

13 MARCH   **1801**   Fourteen-year-old William Marshall, a schoolboy from Southwell, believed he had hit upon the perfect way to get rich quick. After listening at doors he had discovered that Bridget Pigot, who lived in a house beside the Minster, was about to receive a letter from London containing a large amount of money – and he knew just when that letter was due to arrive. Well aware of the route the deliveryman took, he lay in wait, caught him on the highway, robbed him and ran away with his prize. Unfortunately for Marshall there was a serious flaw in his plan: he was local and well known, even to the man delivering the letter. Caught within hours, before he had been able to spend the £54 he had stolen, he was brought to Nottingham and put before the judge. He was found guilty and the court, despite his youth, sentenced him to death.

14 MARCH   **1800**   John Atkinson stood in the dock at Nottingham Assize Court before the Honourable Baron Chambre and pleaded not guilty to the charge of attempting to pass a counterfeit £1 note. A married man, Atkinson owned a shop in Newark, which his wife ran while he travelled around the county as a hawker and peddler. The partnership was certainly successful: the business did extremely well and the second income from his various travels further swelled the family coffers. But Atkinson was a greedy man. At some point the previous year he had come across an accomplished forger by the name of Whittaker. The two men struck a deal and Atkinson began to use Whittaker's counterfeit notes in his transactions with clients all around Nottinghamshire. Shops in Stapleford, Eastwood, Beeston and as far away as Ilkeston all began to discover fake £1 notes in their takings and the finger of suspicion soon pointed firmly in Atkinson's direction. Eventually caught and hauled before the court, he acknowledged his involvement, remarking that he had done it in order to increase his own profit. He added that he believed the offence was relatively insignificant. But forgery, he discovered to his horror, was in fact a capital offence and he was sentenced to death along with Whittaker.

15 MARCH   **1685**   Nottingham's most famous highwayman, John ('Swift Nick') Nevison, was executed on this day. Widely believed to have been the man who made the famous London to York ride that was later credited to Dick Turpin, he and his gang of six robbers operated around Newark using the Talbot Inn as their base. Betrayed in 1676 by a woman named Elizabeth Burton, Nevison escaped the noose by the skin of his teeth and instead was sentenced to transportation to Tangiers. But somehow he was back in Nottinghamshire by 1681. The notoriety he gained at this time derived from no less a person than the king himself. Tired of the constant reports of his nefarious activities Charles II dubbed him 'Swift Nick', because no one had succeeded in catching him. He even put up a reward for his arrest. It took four years but his capture was, of course, inevitable and when it came the court showed no mercy.

1824 Thomas Clever (aged 19) failed to live up to his surname when he was arrested for assaulting a man at Gedling, Nottingham, and stealing from him 2s 6d. The court saw nothing clever in it either and sentenced the poor man to death.

1821 Found guilty of stealing three penknives from Francis Westby's shop in Retford, 17-year-old Frederick Jones was sentenced to be whipped and then imprisoned for three months in Southwell gaol.

1832 A Cry of Murder! Joiner Thomas Popple (aged 40) had shown no outward signs of violence toward his wife and family throughout their married life, but when the elder of his two sons died of smallpox something inside him appeared to snap. During the three weeks following the boy's tragic death, his natural optimism was overwhelmed by deep depression. According to their neighbours, his wife had become ever more fretful over his mental state. She had good reason to be afraid. A broadsheet, published on this day and sold around the city, described how Popple had risen from his bed in the early hours of January morning and attacked his wife with a chisel as she slept. So violent was the attack that he managed to separate the front of her skull from the rest of her head. He then dragged his other son, just, three years old and by this time wide awake, from his bed by his feet. Repeatedly smashing the child's head upon the floor until he was dead, he then simply threw the body on top of that of his wife. Screams of murder from the houses around brought out the night watch and Popple was captured as he ran out into the street screaming.

An artist's impression of Swift Nick and the woman that betrayed him.

SHEEP STEALING.

Twenty Guineas
REWARD.

WHEREAS,

On Saturday Night last the 22nd, or early on Sunday Morning the 23rd day of September instant, a CLOSE in the Occupation of Mr. JOHN KITCHEN, situate in STOKE BARDOLPH, near Ratcliffe Ferry, was entered and

ONE LAMB,

his property, was feloniously slaughtered, and (with the exception of the skin and entrails) stolen and carried away.

Any Person or Persons giving Information so that the Offender or Offenders may be convicted, shall, on such Conviction, receive a

REWARD OF TEN GUINEAS

from the said John Kitchen, and a further

REWARD OF TEN GUINEAS

on application to Messrs. LEESON & GELL, Treasurers to the Association of the Right Honourable EARL MANVERS and his Tenants for the Prosecution of Felons.

And if two or more were concerned, and one will impeach his Accomplice or Accomplices, so that he or they may be convicted, the person so impeaching shall on such conviction be entitled to the above Rewards, and every endeavour shall be used to obtain his Pardon.

NOTTINGHAM, 24th SEPTEMBER, 1832.

J. STAVELEY, PRINTER, NOTTINGHAM.

A reward poster for a lamb published by Nottingham Town in 1832. (Nottingham Local Studies Library)

Retford Town Hall today.

1823 Thomas Roe (aged 21), Benjamin Miller (21) and William Brookes (19) were all found guilty at Nottingham of committing highway robbery in October of the previous year and stealing a silver watch, a steel watch chain, 2s and a neckerchief. Brookes confessed to the robbery, thereby implicating the other two who had consistently denied their involvement. In return for his confession Brookes was freed, while the other two were sentenced to hang.

19 MARCH

1775 Executed on this day was 19-year-old William Voce, a young man whose destiny had been foretold long before. Son of a shoemaker father, he was born in Sneinton but his mother had run away from the family home, taking the boy with her, after a visit to a fortune-teller. The augury she had received predicted there would be a death in her family – and that death would be on a public scaffold; someone was to die by the hand of an executioner and that someone was to be her son. William at that time was only six months old and perhaps understandably his mother refused

20 MARCH

to believe the prophecy. Neighbours who witnessed the sitting agreed with her, convincing her that the fortune teller had been wrong, that it could not possibly be the babe in arms that was to die. It must mean her husband. Without further ado she took young William to Narrow Marsh, where she eventually met and married a man named John Wegdale and began a new life. But the shadow of the fortune-teller forever loomed large, and after her son's arrest for the murder of a young woman, Mary Dufty, at Sneinton she must have known the die was cast.

21 MARCH

1806 At Nottingham's spring assizes 21-year-old William Davies, alias Rhodes, was found guilty of having forged £208 in notes, all of which were found on his person when he was arrested in January. A skilled thief, if not a very successful one, he should at this time have been in Australia, serving out a seven-year sentence, but he had escaped from a prison hulk moored at Portsmouth before he could be transported. Changing his name to Davies, he had returned to his native town and served out an apprenticeship as a forger; as with his thieving exploits of the past, it was not a successful career move. The judge showed no mercy and sentenced him to death. He was executed five days later.

22 MARCH

1822 Henry Sanderson (aged 31) was executed on this day for the murder of William Carr. Born in Carlton, Nottingham, his first job saw him working as a nurseryman alongside his father, and until the age of 14 nothing his

A line drawing of an execution outside Nottingham's Shire Hall.

family ever witnessed suggested that he would end his life on the gallows. Little did they know when they introduced him to the use of guns at that young age that his life would take such a tragic turn. At this time guns were in common use in the countryside, often to poach game, and Henry developed a lethal talent in this direction, despite poaching being a criminal offence for which the penalties were often severe. After his marriage in 1812 Henry lived for a short while in Bawtry, where his shooting skills were put to good use providing most of the meat that reached his table. When he returned to Carlton in 1821 he saw no reason to change his habits, as poaching had become a way of life for him. In October 1821 he took his trusty gun into the woodland near his home to shoot some rabbits. Unfortunately he was seen by the gamekeeper, William Carr, who tried to catch him. A scuffle ensued and Henry was quickly overpowered but not disarmed. He asked the gamekeeper to release him, and when he refused Henry pushed the barrel of his gun beneath the keeper's waistcoat and shot him. Carr was later found and carried out of the wood; he lived for a further agonising twenty-four hours during which time he managed to give a full statement. Henry was clearly identified as the poacher and the killer.

One of the entrances to Nottingham's Shire Hall.

1785 The execution of John Pendrill and John Townsend took place before a huge crowd. Widely publicised before his trial, Pendrill's family history had proved fascinating to the people of Nottingham. He was one of the Pendrills of Staffordshire, a family that had gained worldwide fame after concealing

23 MARCH

Charles II from Cromwell's Parliamentarians after his ignominious defeat at the battle of Worcester over a century earlier. Their reputation had been hard won and was greatly envied by many, but it clearly meant little to the man who mounted the scaffold on this day. According to broadsheets circulated after his death, Pendrill had formed a criminal alliance with Townsend, and in January of this same year the two had attacked Edwalton farmer William Vinson at West Bridgeford. After initially escaping with 23s in silver coin, a silver watch and a quantity of tea, sugar, soap and tobacco, they were cornered and captured on Trent Bridge. At the trial Mr Justice Heath, who had a fearsome reputation for severity, told the two: 'I will cause the laws to be executed with such severity as shall enable any gentleman to hang his watch by the highway side, with full confidence of finding it there on his return another day!'

24 MARCH **1681** Robert Sharbrook, a middle-aged beggar from Derby, was sentenced to be whipped by Mansfield churchwardens 'for wandering as a rogue', and then was to be allowed two days to travel back to his home where he was ordered to remain or face a second public whipping.

25 MARCH **1795** On this day 36-year-old David Proctor, a former sailor in the Royal Navy, climbed the steps to the gallows in Nottingham before a huge jeering crowd. He had been found guilty of the rape of Charlotte Hemms, alias Waters, his 10-year-old sister-in-law, although he never admitted his guilt.

26 MARCH **1806** Tom Otter was executed for the murder of his wife on their wedding night. His body was later hung in chains from a gibbet at a place known as Byards Leap.

27 MARCH **1893** Crowds lined the roadside around Bagthorpe prison, in places four or five deep, waiting for the black flag to be hoisted signifying the execution of Walter Smith. Days earlier members of that same crowd had signed a petition attempting to obtain a reprieve for a man many thought innocent of the murder for which he would hang. An inventor, Smith had set up Abbott's Factory in Hyson Green, Nottingham, where he had perfected, refined and patented a machine capable of producing coloured chenille and a variety of other materials allied to ladies' fashion. By the start of the 1890s he had also become an enthusiastic cyclist, and had begun to refine the designs of bicycles. Into this world stepped Catherine Cross, an attractive 24-year-old nurse working in Liverpool's women's hospital. In November 1892 she arrived at her parents' Nottingham home for a two-week holiday. In need of a new dress she had gone to Smith's house to meet his mother Harriett, a capable dressmaker, and here she met Walter over a cup of tea. He invited her to see his factory, and a day or so later she duly arrived at Hyson Green at a little after 11 a.m. She could not have known when she entered the machine-shop that Walter Smith was armed with a gun he had bought the day before. As she looked at the chenille machine Smith shot her. Badly wounded, she ran from the workshop and collapsed in the street; she died as a result of the

The BIRTH, LIFE
PARENTAGE,
TRIAL,
Condemnation,
AND
BEHAVIOUR,
OF

Who was executed upon
Nottingham Gallows,
On Wednesday, March 25,
1795,
FOR A
RAPE
On CHARLOTTE WATERS
His Daughter-in-Law,
An Infant under the age of 10 years.

DAVID PROCTOR, aged 36,

MANKIND having now arrived at the utmost stretch of their prerogative ordained by the fore-knowledge of God, a free agency in all things, we fee in the world conspicuous evidences of Virtue as well as Vice; but the radiance of the former being so exceedingly heightened by the immunity of the latter, that the good and pious man is often seen both to smile and weep, almost at the same moment. In the case before us, we have a species of Vice to unfold, (to quote the words of the Ghost in a particular part of HAMLET) "That will freeze thy young blood, and make each particular hair to stand "on end like quills of the affrighted Porcupine, &c.";—indeed, to extenuate the offence, is impossible; we wish there was room for palliation, but the impenitence of the person involved precludes any favourable report.

What tongue can express, or imagination paint, the heart-rending grief and poignant sorrow of the real parents of this child, had they been alive to have witnessed such a nefarious deed by any one; but with what astonishment and concern will the world be informed, that a nominal parent, at least was the man who could transgress the Laws of Nature as well as his Country; and, "Oh! Shame, where is thy blush," who could pollute the body of an innocent child with a certain disease, that's but too prevalent in the world! Reader, does not this excite indignant sensations in thy breast? Yes, but the sentence of the Law awaiting the guilty, especially this guilty person, a part of that indignation becomes suppressed, and another kind of sensation takes place, namely, that of Pity, he had no more grace. But then he ought to have been the protector, not the seducer, of the child left to his care?—Granted; but if reason and religion were far from his heart, if education and instruction were neglected him in his youth, and a sense of honour had never been instilled into his breast, is there not a small crevice for human fallibility to creep through; and human kindness to sympathize? Yes, in commending the Sinner to the mercy of an all-wise and gracious Creator of all things, "who best knowing our infirmities" will allot us such portions in his heavenly kingdom, as our works here on earth shall have deserved.

The ties of our common nature might have stept in, and secretly whispered to him that it was unnatural in the extreme; is the brief answer to the foregoing but necessary interrogatories; Conscience was not awake; the Man and the Parent were extinct; Lust and Filthiness alone had dominion over his mind, that chained him down to the rude and barbarous notion of cleansing his abominable impurities by the forced connections with an innocent baby! Blush, all ye seducers of female virtue! Ye gay and thoughtless! Rouse from your venereal pleasures, take a view of this case, and ask yourselves what degree of difference there is between it and yours? That it is wide from it, we must admit; but a continuation in your way makes the heart callous, and utterly insensible to the joys of a more refined and excellent understanding. Ye Libertines of every Country! rouse from your filthy embraces, and become converts to genuine love; that pure love for the sex's greatness, that will make you ashamed of a further prosecution so detrimental to true honour; see, what a terrible exemple is before your eyes; awake, then, at the voice of Truth, lay down your carnal warfare, and gird yourselves with the weapons of spiritual conviction, that you may triumph over the Lust and Dominion of Satan, and be received as conquerors "through Him who loved us."

TRIAL and SENTENCE of DAVID PROCTOR, Cutler.

AT the Assizes held at the Guildhall of the Town of NOTTINGHAM, on Friday the 13th of March, 1795, before the Hon. Sir GILES ROOKE, Knt. one of his Majesty's Justices of the Court of Common Pleas, the unhappy prisoner, DAVID PROCTOR, at a quarter past six in the morning, was put to the bar, and arraigned on an indictment for committing a Rape on the body of CHARLOTTE WATERS, his Daughter in-law, an infant under the age of ten years, in September last, and her did carnally know and abuse against the form of the Statute in that case made and provided—He pleaded not guilty to the indictment, on which the learned Judge proceeded to examine evidence; and first the child herself:

"My child, has any body explained to you the nature of an Oath, and do you know that you are come here to speak the truth?" Yes, I will tell the truth, said the little innocent. "Where do you expect to go to, if you do not, then, tell every thing you know what your father did to you?" To the Bad Man, replied the child. "Well, then, my Dear, what did he say to you when he first offered violence?" *He would kill me if I made any noise.* "How often did he repeat those naughty tricks?" *A many times, Sir.* "When did you perceive yourself ill after he had done such a wicked thing?" *Some weeks after.* "How came it at last to be known, my child?"—*I told a woman I'd got the belly ach, and she gave me something for it; but she said my breath was not right, and she would send for a Doctor.* [Here the deposition of the Surgeon was taken.]

The circumstances of his examination are too shocking to meet the public attention on paper, but he abundantly proved the veracity of the girl's evidence; her tale was artless, and her deportment in this trying situation spoke conviction to the minds of all present, except the prisoner's, who endeavoured to transfer the blame from himself to a man of the name of Waterman, who

sometimes came to his house, and slept there. And here is certainly an exaggeration of his offence, by wishing to involve an intimate acquaintance in the same trouble. The child proved that this man never came up stairs, but slept on two chairs below. This plea of the prisoner, which he alledged in defence, was considered by the Court and Jury as vague and unsatisfactory, and could not be taken as exculpatory. The evidence being closed, Mr. Justice Rooke briefly recapitulated it, and then left the whole with the Jury, who, after a few minutes' consultation, found David Proctor guilty of the crime laid to his charge. Proclamation for silence being made, the Judge addressed the prisoner in a most awful and impressive manner, pointing out, in pathetic terms, the remarkable heinousness of his offence, and the just punishment annexed to it; and conjured him to make every suitable ejaculation to he Author of his existence, to pardon his multiplied iniquities, to shed his influential spirit of grace upon his heart and mind, that he might obtain that mercy from above, which human laws had made it necessary as a warning to others, could not be expected here; & which, too, the Royal Clemency could not be petitioned for in this instance. Sorry are we to remark, that the prisoner treated both the admonition and the sentence with an obduracy not very common to men in his dreadful situation, who told the Judge that what he had passed upon him was " real murder." The whole Court were shocked at his behaviour; indeed, throughout the trial, there was a continued sentiment of detestation of the circumstances as they arose, which might have pierced the heart of any other man but the prisoner's.

His BIRTH and PARENTAGE.

He was about 36 years of age, born in London, brought up with his father as a Cutler, and lived with him till he was about twenty years of age, and then went on board a man of war, where he continued three years in the marine service. Soon after, he came to this town, where he followed the occupation of a Razor Grinder about the streets and neighbouring villages. He has two sisters living in London, one of whom keeps a livery-stable in Fetter-Lane: he has also two uncles resident at Sheffield, one of whom is in a very capital line of life.

His BEHAVIOUR after CONDEMNATION.

One would naturally conclude, that the obduracy of his manners would have softened some hours after sentence was passed, and that reflection, with the melting persuasions of the Reverend Chaplain who attended him, had operated powerfully to work upon his feelings a sense of contrition; but, alas! the hour was not yet come when he would burst out in lamentations, the spirit of grace had not expanded its benign influence upon him; much remained to be done; here's a Sinner between earth and heaven, between heaven and hell! Thus is his condition painted for the whole of the last week: no confession of his fault would he make: otherwise, his demeanour was decent and regular to those who attended him, but very reserved, and desired no assistance from any persons of religious persuasions but the Rev. Chaplain aforesaid, who attends the prisoners in the county-goal, and who has been very assiduous in his visits to him on this occasion.

Mercy, O Lord, extend to him who is in chains so bound,
Loosen his fetters, that the Sinner may no longer be found!

TUESDAY, March 24.— This afternoon the Reverend Chaplain, again visited him, and was concerned to find no impression for the better. He still persisted in denying that he committed the crime for which he was about to be precipitated to an ignominious death and an untimely grave.— Unhappy and mistaken man, Humanity may plead in vain to recal thee to thyself! the beneficent endeavours to contrast the joys of a heavenly state to the horrid prospect of that wretched one, where the fire that never quencheth," will be lost, lost for ever, in a short space, if thou turnest not quickly; but the gates are open even at the last hour—" There is more joy over one sinner that repenteth, than over ninety and nine just persons."

WEDNESDAY morning - Impenitent still; the cavalcade, however, was ordered to form, and the usual means got ready to conduct the unhappy man to execution: when an unusual multitude had assembled by half past 10 o'clock to join the procession, which began to move about eleven, and proceeded slowly through the streets to the fatal tree; where being arrived, he knelt down on his coffin, and joined in prayer with the Chaplain; at the conclusion, the latter again pressed him to declare and confess his guilt, describing him how terrible a thing it was to go out of the world with a lie in his mouth. The executioner then proceeded to do his office, and a dead silence reigned throughout the whole assemblage; at length the moment arrived that was to terminate his existence and just as he was turning off, he was heard to utter, " Lord have mercy on me, I'm, Im'——" Thus finished a life which might have ended full of honour and length of days, if in his youth he had been tutored with wholesome correction; and hence appears the great necessity of National Schools, that would make this kind the glory of the earth.

Broadsheet detailing the execution of David Proctor, 1795. (Nottingham Local Studies Library)

gunshot wound two weeks later. Smith was arrested and, despite Catherine's dying statement that the shooting had been an accident, he was found guilty of murder.

28 MARCH 1781 George Brown, a 36-year-old labourer, and his good friend Adam Bagshaw paid a heavy price for the burglaries the two had carried out in Nottingham and Derby during the previous year. Both were executed before an unforgiving crowd at precisely half past twelve in the afternoon.

29 MARCH 1905 The jury took only twenty minutes to decide that 29-year-old John Hutchinson was guilty of the horrific murder of little Albert Matthews. Hutchinson lodged with the Matthews family at a house in Narrow Marsh, Nottingham, paying rent when he could afford to and looking after the Matthews' son if his parents needed to go out. On the evening of 31 January Rose Matthews, Albert's mother, asked Hutchinson if he would put the boy to bed because she needed to go out and her husband was not due to return until later. Hutchinson agreed but when the boy would not stop crying he first battered him with a poker, then strangled him to death and finally cut off the child's head before mutilating the body. Leaving the remains where they lay, he had then left the house and gone out drinking. He was executed at eight in the morning by Britain's executioner John Billington.

30 MARCH 1774 This day saw the execution of Robert Wheatley (aged 35), one of Nottingham's most prolific robbers. Caught after stealing seven dozen stockings from the bleach yard of Unwin & Sons at Sutton in Ashfield, it was discovered while he languished in prison that he was the same Robert Wheatley who had escaped from a prison ship taking him in chains to America in 1767 after being sentenced that year for a similar crime. The courts took a dim view of transported prisoners who returned to England without serving out their sentence and Wheatley knew that he would be harshly treated, but he did not expect to be sentenced to death. That verdict came about because he was strongly suspected of having murdered a woman in Basford. Whether guilty or not, he accepted the verdict and before being pushed off the cart that had carried him to the hangman he addressed the huge and cheering crowd, pleading with them to 'follow the teachings of the church and obey the Sabbath'.

31 MARCH 1802 Notorious highwayman Ferdinando Davis (aged 24) mounted the scaffold at a little after midday. He had been found guilty of robbing a man of 100 guineas, and embarking upon a criminal career that saw him commit robberies at Lenton, Trent Bridge, Caythorpe and Hoveringham. Before leaping from the cart he shook hands with all those around him before turning to his young, inexperienced executioner and telling him loudly, 'Do you also take warning, the Lord forgive both you and I.' At that point the crowds fell strangely silent and as he launched himself into eternity they gave as one a shriek of horror.

APRIL

A gibbetted body, normally hung at a crossroads
as a warning to others, mid-eighteenth century.

1 APRIL **1807** Robert Barlow Cook (aged 27) had intended to marry his long-time sweetheart Sarah Sandaver within a year of their first meeting but he had been struck down by consumption. Despite the seriousness of his illness and his growing incapacity the two remained loyal to each other. Sarah, all too well aware of the nature of the disease, steadfastly refused to leave his side and nursed him through his gradual decline. When doctors finally declared that his life was coming to a close and there was nothing else that could be done, he asked her a second time if she would marry him. Her answer was a determined yes, and this day was chosen for the wedding. With difficulty Cook rose early from his bed, dressed with the aid of friends, and with the support of his intended brother-in-law walked slowly and painfully to Southwell Minster. There, before a huge assembly of family and friends, he and Sarah stood side by side and made their wedding vows to each other. But before the priest could make the entry into the marriage book Robert Cook sank slowly to his knees and died in the arms of his new bride.

2 APRIL **1823** On this day Thomas Roe and Benjamin Miller were executed in Nottingham. Both men had been convicted after the third member of their gang, Thomas Brookes, turned approver and gave evidence against them. All three had taken part in a violent robbery on the Mansfield road five months earlier, which had left labourer Samuel Marriott badly beaten. At the trial the court was told that the attack was a purely random affair: after a night's drinking the three had made a drunken pact to attack the first man they saw. Unfortunately for Marriott he was in the wrong place at the wrong time, and all they got for their trouble was a 2s piece, an old pocket watch and chain, and a neckerchief.

3 APRIL **1818** On this day William Mandeville (aged 22) and George Needham (25) were executed for the crime of burglary. Eight months earlier they had broken into the house of Samuel Hough at Burton Joyce. After threatening to slit his throat, they had made off with a significant quantity of linen and women's clothing. Unfortunately for the duo one of the men had used the name 'Dick' during the robbery and police knew that Mandeville, apart from having a history of burglary to his name, was known locally as 'Waggoner Dick', a nickname acquired after years spent managing a team of horses hauling wagons between Nottingham and Southwell. He was seen later the following day in conversation with two women, one of whom was the sister of Nottingham's notorious robber, George Bates; the police needed no further proof. They searched the two women's homes and found a gown and shift known to have belonged to the household at Burton Joyce. Both men escaped to Newark, where Needham was later arrested and found to be in possession of all the linen that had been stolen. Mandeville was caught a few weeks later after having removed an entire shop window in Thurgarton to steal shoes.

1827 Caught in the Act! Highwayman William Wells was caught trying to escape after robbing Basford shoemaker, Joseph Cordin of 2 sovereigns, a half-crown, a few shillings, a sixpence and a watch. There was no doubt about his guilt but Wells made a full confession, and also admitted to having been a horse thief for years. He travelled to the scaffold in a cart with his eyes firmly closed all the way. The following day a remorseful poem was circulated through the city, although it is not known if it was truly written by the condemned man.

4 APRIL

> In this dark cell, where many a wretch like me,
> Has breathed in sighs his misery,
> In this lone place, a prey to keen despair,
> O Lord, my God, come listen to my prayer.
> Tho' by foul deeds such sinners thee provoke,
> Suffer me, thy name for mercy to invoke,
> And whilst I live, tho' late condemned to die,
> Cast toward my sins a kind indulgent eye.
> Sincerely I repent, O let me be forgiv'n,
> And tho' unworthy see thy face in heaven;
> Turn not away, but mark my inward grief,
> And look on me as on the humble thief.
> With tears and moans I ask my God of thee,
> To save my soul when from the fatal tree,
> Life's spark is fled, and I must then appear,
> I know not how! Alas, I know not where.

1808 Robert Calvin was found guilty at the assizes of the gross abuse of two young girls and was ordered by the court to be placed in the stocks in Nottingham's market place for a period of one hour and then returned to prison. He therefore became the first person to receive such a sentence for sixty years and attained the dubious honour of being the last man ever placed in Nottingham's stocks. Immense crowds turned out to see Calvin's public humiliation, despite heavy rain throughout the hour, but were disappointed and angry at being denied the age-old custom of retribution. A strong body of constables and the presence of the 45th Regiment of Foot ensured that he sustained no injury during his brief incarceration in the stocks, the crowd being allowed to hurl nothing more than verbal abuse. After his release Calvin bowed to the mob before being placed in a cart and returned to prison. No doubt he was relieved to have escaped without serious injury.

5 APRIL

A drawing of stocks as they would have appeared in the nineteenth century.

6 APRIL 1752 The body of James Wogden, known to those who knew him as 'innocent Jemmy', was handed over to Nottingham doctors to be dissected following his execution before a large crowd two days earlier. Despite his protestations of innocence, he had been found guilty of having brutally murdered Edward Whatman at Ollerton earlier in the year. Whether the nickname had anything to do with his trial and subsequent conviction is unclear.

A nineteenth-century drawing of men viewing the deceased.

7 APRIL 1735 Labourer Henry Parnell, a native of Cotgrave and an extremely unsavoury character, murdered his wife after a night's drinking. Incensed that she had had the temerity to retire to bed instead of waiting up for him, he created so much noise outside the house that she was forced to go downstairs and let him in. He then beat her because there was no candle to light the house, and sent her off to borrow one from neighbours. Threatened with further violence and not wanting to provoke his anger further, she did as asked. Unfortunately for her, when she returned he attacked her the minute she pushed open the door. After beating her a second time he threw her to the floor, sat upon her chest and applied so much pressure that her back broke, killing her instantly. At the coroner's inquest held the following day it was decided by the jury that she had 'Died by the visitation of God'. Parnell was not to be charged. Villagers rose up in anger and insisted that a second jury be formed and that Parnell be judged for the crime. This time the verdict was unanimous: guilty of wilful murder. The obnoxious Henry Parnell was executed three weeks later before a loud and jeering crowd.

8 APRIL 1908 Mansfield tattooist Arthur Scott attacked a customer after he refused to pay. Charlie Mills ran from the shop after having his arm tattooed and it took two days for Scott to track him down. After spotting him in Mansfield's market place he followed him home and attempted to shoot him. Mills escaped but was caught again twenty-four hours later and slashed across the

face with a penknife. Unfortunately for Scott, though, tattoo artists were rare in Mansfield and so he was not difficult to find. He was quickly tracked down and arrested, and the magistrates sent him to prison for one month's hard labour.

1844 After a night in the village pub William Boot (aged 18), James Smith (19), Peter Alford (20) and James Wild (23) decided to commit a burglary. They chose the home of George Clark in Sutton in Ashfield, a place they knew well – but also a place where they were equally well known. The whole escapade was a disaster from the start. They managed to escape with 7*d* but were seen and recognised as they left and were arrested within hours. For their brief excursion into crime all three were sentenced to be transported for fifteen years.

9 APRIL

1805 'The confession of Robert Powell' was printed and sold to the crowds who flocked to Nottingham to witness his execution. A baker by trade, Powell had turned to crime after the early death of his wife. He formed a partnership with a Sheffield publican named Cooper and together they carried out a number of daring robberies across the county before finally being captured in Worksop. There the two had robbed James Leeming, a day labourer, of his life savings, which amounted to 38 gold guineas, 5 half-guineas and a 7-shilling piece, but the pair had been unable to make an effective escape. Powell, alias Harvey, had no hesitation in confessing his guilt and at the trial of both men the judge handed down sentences of death. Cooper was later reprieved, but Powell was deemed to have committed the worse offence – he had threatened Leeming with a loaded and primed pistol – and the law was ordered to take its course. From his prison cell he dictated the details of his life, which publishers rushed to print in order to sell it as he made the journey to the gallows.

10 APRIL

1909 An inquest held at Leen Side, Nottingham, heard how Lambley framework knitter William Skinner (aged 51) had wandered into the path of a tram on Carrington Street. As he crossed the road to go for a drink in the Alexander Hotel, he ignored the warning bells of the approaching tram, which was travelling at only 10 miles an hour. He was hit head-on and died instantly.

11 APRIL

1613 Robert Key and Elizabeth Lamyng, both of Ratcliffe, were placed in the stocks before Sunday service, stripped to the waist and whipped. Their crime is not recorded, but they were forced to remain there for three hours. After the service they were joined by Helen Beardsley, who had been found guilty of petty larceny.

12 APRIL

A drawing of stocks which doubled as a whipping post.

1701 On this day 29-year-old Timothy Buckley was executed at Nottingham's Gallows Hill. Born in Stanford

13 APRIL

to wealthy parents, he had chosen to leave home to pursue a career as a highwayman. He was accomplished in his chosen profession but he made a critically serious error when he attempted to rob a coach on the Derby–Nottingham road, some 2 miles outside Nottingham. Inside were three gentlemen of Nottingham, and two footmen all armed with a number of weapons. They refused to yield to Buckley's demands and a gun battle ensued. Firing a blunderbuss through the coach's open window, one of the men managed to bring down Buckley's horse, and over the next few minutes the young highwayman fired off all eight of his pistols, killing one of the gentlemen and a footman. But Buckley himself was hit eleven times. Weak from loss of blood and out of shot, he eventually collapsed and was captured. At his trial there was little choice but to admit his guilt and thousands turned out to watch as the cart carrying him to his execution travelled through the city.

14 APRIL   **1911 Tragedy on the Trent** Thomas Barks took his wife, who was recovering from a recent operation, and two small children for a trip on his barge along the Trent Navigation canal. The day went well until they approached a bridge where the water was flowing faster than normal. Barks was unable to manoeuvre the boat fast enough to pass under an arch of the bridge, and the barge's port bow struck the brickwork, forcing the bow downwards and allowing water to pour across the deck. At the time of the collision his wife was sitting beside an open hatchway cradling the youngest of their children, 3-year-old Eric. Realising they were about to be swept away he made a dash toward them but just as he reached them the barge capsized and everyone was thrown into the river. Barks only had time to seize his second child, George, before the barge rolled over on top of the family. Barks and George managed to swim to the surface and were rescued but his wife and little Eric stood no chance. Unable to swim out from beneath the overturned barge, they were trapped as it began to settle in the water. On the canal side Barks could only watch in despair as the barge slowly sank to the bottom of the canal basin, his wife and son still fighting to escape. Their bodies were recovered a short time later.

15 APRIL   **1885** Arthur Dart, an unemployed Nottingham labourer, made his seventh appearance in court in as many years and was sentenced to twelve months' hard labour for stealing a pair of slippers, some paintbrushes and a tin of salmon, which he had attempted to sell at Sneinton market.

16 APRIL   **1936** At exactly 9 a.m. Nottingham nurse Dorothea Nancy Waddingham was executed for the murder of Ada Baguley. The case had caused a huge sensation across the country. Waddingham had admitted Ada into her Nottingham care home and then carefully planned the woman's death. The motive was money. Waddingham knew that Ada Baguley, a 50-year-old woman in very poor health, had inherited both capital and property from her father. Over a period of eight months she managed to force the poor woman

MORPHIA ORDERED FOR PATIENTS IN HOME

Headline relating to the Dorothy Waddingham case. *(Nottingham Evening Post)*

"Unused Tablets Returned By Accused Nurse" | Couple Face Poison Plot Accusation

DEAD WOMAN'S INCURABLE ILLNESS EXPLAINED

Two Nottingham doctors gave the chief evidence when the Nottingham home murder trial was resumed at the Shire Hall to-day. The hearing is now expected to last for most of the week.

The prisoners are Dorothea Nancy Waddingham, 34, and Ronald Joseph Sullivan, 41, and they have pleaded not guilty to having wilfully murdered (by administering poison) Miss Ada Louisa Baguley, 50, daughter of Mrs. Louisa Baguley, 87, whose late husband was a shoemaker at Burton Joyce.

Both women died at 32, Devon-drive, Sherwood, a home kept by Waddingham, assisted by Sullivan.

Evidence to-day was given by Dr. Jacob and Dr. Manfield. Dr. Jacob described Miss Baguley's incurable disease. He was questioned about her expectation of life.

DR. MANFIELD AND DRUGS

Dr Manfield told the jury of drugs he prescribed for patients at the Devon-drive home. After one patient died tablets were returned to him by Waddingham. They were returned voluntarily, and he was satisfied they represented what she had left.

In reply to questions, the doctor told the court that he had given tablets—more than 100, he said—from his pocket to Waddingham for patients. The tablets were given from time to time, and were half-grain morphia tablets.

Dr. Manfield denied advising Waddingham to say nothing about giving morphia tablets to Ada Baguley. He also denied saying that if it became necessary, he would deal with the matter.

Nottm. Undertaker Questioned About Cremation

THE crowd outside the Shire Hall was not as great as it was yesterday. This was not due to any diminution of interest in the case, but because more tickets had been issued

Counsel In The Case

FOR THE CROWN.
Mr. P. Birkett, K.C., and Mr.

FOR WADDINGHAM.
Mr J. F. Eales, K.C., M.P., and Mr. Wm Smith.

FOR SULLIVAN.
Mr. A. m. Lyons, K.C., M.P., Mr John Smith.

Mr. R. A. Young is instructing counsel for the defence.

seats in court. These numbered about 150. The two galleries were seated

cremation that has to be done and the undertaker has to have certain documents I understand so

Mr said he had calling at whole of the that the prisoners had been there and seen Miss Baguley many times.

She undoubtedly way physically he saw Sullivan the house making up fires and sweeping

Mr Lyons · Every time you clear that his position house one of the domestic help?—I should say so.

Lyons. It could be said on any occasion that he was in control of anybody household?— agree.

suppose you saw no association between Miss Baguley and Sullivan? not He was merely doing things about house

Witness said his business at took only a couple of minutes on each of weekly visits. He called to collect premiums on life insurance policy on both Sullivan Waddingham paid the money rule. He only Mrs Baguley occasionally.

Cremation Forms

an

Later witness went to 32. Devon drive and saw some incomplete papers. These were delivered to him the next morning in completed form

He took them to Wilford Hill Cemetery and paid the necessary fees.

Mr. Lyons. Am I right in saying that Sullivan was told by you what had to be done? That is so.

A two days interval for burial was quite reasonable time.

He saw the body of Miss Baguley.

She was a woman who had of suffering for a long time.

expressed the view it was the kind case where cremation undoubtedly advisable?· It discussed.

She had You did say a body fit for body

Jacob's Story

Well, any body is, but particular body saw was certainly subject?—Yes weighty, about 17 stones.

Witness she had undergone.

Does the question of patient not affect question of cremation at all

Dr. F. H. Jacob, 52 Regent-street, No

to change her will, making herself the key beneficiary of this wealth. She then administered an overdose of morphine that killed Ada. A routine post-mortem found over 3 grams in the woman's body, and the police were able to stop the hastily arranged cremation from going ahead. At the trial it was also revealed that the only nursing experience Waddingham had ever had was as a maid at the infirmary at Burton-on-Trent. The verdict of guilty was greeted by uproar in some quarters and petitions were raised in an attempt to obtain a reprieve. As the clock began to strike the hour the huge crowd that had gathered outside the prison gates sang 'Abide with me'.

17 APRIL **1800** A report in the Nottingham Date Book records that the gallows, two uprights and a transverse beam approximately 12ft high, which stood on the summit of the hill beside the Nottingham–Mansfield road, had been stolen.

18 APRIL **1903** A body found in a field at Farndon, near Newark, was identified from letters he had been carrying as Harry Clarke (aged 38), a native of Newark. His throat had been cut with a razor, which was found beside the body. An inquest at the Britannia Inn, Farndon, heard evidence that Clarke had served with the Sherwood Rangers Yeomanry in the Boer War, during which time he had contracted enteric fever, which had affected his mind. Police were satisfied that no one else had been involved in his death and the coroner returned a verdict of 'suicide whilst suffering temporary insanity'.

19 APRIL **1885** Charles Mitchell (aged 39) stood in the dock at Nottingham's courthouse and pleaded not guilty to the charge of bigamy. His second wife, Mary Bland, had been persuaded to marry him after he had produced a funeral card announcing the death of his first wife Lucy, whom he said was buried in Leicester. He also had a letter, purportedly from his brother-in-law, who was by this time conveniently in Australia, offering up his commiser-ations at Mitchell's loss. It was all plausible enough to convince both Mary and her family, who knew that Mitchell had married at some time in the late 1870s. Believing that he was indeed a widower, Mary tied the knot at St Mark's Church, Nottingham, in November 1884. The event was well attended. Unfortunately for Mitchell, someone in the wedding party realised that he had lied. Lucy then unexpectedly appeared on the scene, leading to Mitchell's inevitable arrest. In court he insisted that he had never realised that Lucy was still alive, declaring that he had never intended to deceive. The jury refused to believe him and Mr Justice Stephen sentenced him to eight months' hard labour.

20 APRIL **1776** At the Quarter Sessions at Nottingham's Shire Hall, Hannah Mottram of Mansfield pleaded guilty to two charges of petty larceny. She was publicly whipped from the back of a cart in Nottingham's market square the same day.

21 APRIL **1752** Executed at Nottingham on this day was 27-year-old Woolston Roberts. A serving soldier and veteran of the battles of Fontenoy, Val, Falkirk

Main entrance to
the Shire Hall,
Nottingham.

and Culloden, he had been found guilty of robbery. On a furlough from the
army he met his good friend and fellow soldier William Sandham just outside
Nottingham, and the two went for a drink in a nearby public house. Here they
were joined by a stranger, Benjamin Voos. Woolston and Sandham asked
Voos to enlist in the army but he refused. They offered him a shilling as an
inducement and accidentally knocked it onto the floor. Voos bent down to
retrieve it and was told by Woolston that in so doing he had accepted the
King's shilling and must enlist. An argument followed and eventually the two

soldiers left the pub. Voos later insisted that before leaving they had robbed him of 10s. A meeting that had begun so innocently proved very costly for both men. Sandham was executed later.

22 APRIL **1903** An inquest into the death of William Smalley (aged 57) heard evidence from his work colleagues that he had been tragically crushed to death in a grinding mill at Newark. It was his job to clean out the grinding machine before the start of each shift, and he had decided to clear the stones from the main cogwheel just before the afternoon shift began. He told a young mill lad to go and find the engine driver and tell him not to start up the machine until he signalled that all was clear. The lad, however, was distracted on his way to delivering the message and when he finally found the engine driver he had forgotten what he had been told to say. In his confusion he mistakenly told the driver that Smalley had sent him over to tell him to start the engine. Smalley was immediately caught by the suddenly moving cogwheel and dragged into the body of the machine. By the time the mechanism was stopped he had lost both legs and his body was battered to a pulp.

23 APRIL **1685** On this day 28-year-old Joan Phillips was executed on gallows erected at the junction of Loughborough Road and Wilford Lane. The daughter of a respectable Northamptonshire farmer, she had eloped from the family home with her lover Edward Bracy, a man who had falsely claimed to hold a position in society in order to ingratiate himself into her affections. The elopement was a sham; it was later discovered that Joan, under Bracy's influence, had robbed her family of all the money they possessed and the family silver plate. After a series of audacious robberies the couple took a house in Bristol where they enjoyed an extremely lavish lifestyle. To meet their rising costs they became highwaymen. Famous for her great beauty Joan attracted the interest of a number of men, all of whom worked either in or on the edge of the criminal world. None of this went unnoticed by the authorities, and eventually the couple were forced to ride north to escape justice. Joan, dressed as a man, mounted on horseback with pistols in her holsters, took to holding up coaches on the Nottingham and Leicester roads, a dangerous practice which led to her inevitable downfall. Captured after a failed attempt to hold up a coach on the Loughborough road, she readily acknowledged her guilt and accepted her fate. There is no record of what happened to Bracy.

24 APRIL **1773** Nottingham labourer John Green was found guilty of having stolen a cloth coat from a man in Mansfield. He was branded with a hot iron on his right hand and imprisoned for six months.

25 APRIL **1787** Thomas Flanagan was arrested after threatening to kill a constable and while in prison was found to be a wanted man. Two months earlier he had stolen a checked apron after breaking into a house in Mansfield. At his trial he was found guilty and sentenced to seven years' transportation.

Stockwell Gate, Mansfield, *c.* 1912.

1909 After being arrested in March, Albert and Emma Stacy appeared in Mansfield's courthouse charged with gross neglect of their nine children, ranging from two months to nine years old. NSPCC officers had visited their home in December 1908 and found five children without any clothes, three without shoes and the baby lying naked on a dirty bed sucking on a sour and filthy bottle. School inspectors also reported that none of the children had been to school for two months. In the house there were only two beds, each with a mattress but no bed linen, and the mattress used by the children was completely soaked in urine. The court sentenced Albert and Emma to two months' hard labour.

26 APRIL

1812 The Luddites were waiting for William Trentham. Incensed that he intended to cut their wages they wanted him dead. As he arrived home at around a quarter to ten at night two men stepped out from behind tombstones in the churchyard opposite and, without uttering a word, one fired a pistol at him. The ball struck him in the right breast and lodged beneath his shoulder. He was quickly found and local surgeon Mr Pelham succeeded in removing the ball, saving Trentham's life. Nottingham's mayor put up a reward of 100 guineas for anyone that would name the attackers and a further 500 guineas for any conviction. There were no takers and the would-be assassins were never traced though popular belief held that they were executed some years later in Loughborough after taking part in an attack on a Leicester factory.

27 APRIL

1911 The murdered body of a baby was discovered in the River Trent by Police Constable Smithson. According to post-mortem evidence the body had been in the water for at least four weeks and was so decomposed that even the sex could not be stated. With no clothing or other evidence to enable any sort of identification, the verdict was simply one of 'found dead'.

28 APRIL

Market Place, Newark, *c.* 1915.

29 APRIL **1865** On this day 13-year-old Thirza Thorpe was sent to prison for seven days after being found guilty of stealing an iron weight from a coal merchant's yard. Owing to her youth the coal merchant, William Turner, attempted to stop the case and force the withdrawal of the charge but magistrates would have none of it. Prison, they declared, was the only solution to theft, regardless of age.

30 APRIL **1808** Convicted at Newark-upon-Trent Quarter Assizes of stealing a quantity of malt, John Coupe, who was well known to the court for a variety of previous offences, was sentenced to be transported for seven years.

MAY

Nottingham Market Square, *c.* 1900.

1 MAY   1800   The strange gravestone of Nottingham's famous fortune-teller, known only as Mrs Bluff, who died in 1800, stands in St Mary's churchyard and bears the following inscription:

> Here lies Mrs Bluff, who had more than enough
> Of money laid in store,
> And when she died, she shut her eyes,
> And never spoke any more.

2 MAY   1808   Prison records show that the governor of Southwell's house of correction was to be paid £100 a year plus a quarter of all the net profits gained from what was referred to as prisoners' task work. The turnkey (gaoler) was to be paid only 20s a year while the prison chaplain was to receive 20s in return for preaching a sermon every Sunday and attending services on Christmas Day and Good Friday.

3 MAY   1884   **Baffling death at Retford** An inquest opened at the Queens Hotel Retford, into the death of 20-year-old Miss Louisa Emily Plant, the daughter of Retford's lord mayor, whose decapitated body had been found beside the Mansfield to Retford railway line. A graduate of Newnham College Cambridge from where she had received the high honour of being the first female scholar in England, she was a professor of botany and divinity at Sheffield's High School. Her death had proved a mystery to both her family and the police. According to evidence heard by the coroner, she had taken up

All that remains of Southwell's house of correction is this impressive gateway.

her post at Sheffield three days before her death and had returned to Retford to spend the weekend with her father. She was proud of her achievements and there had been nothing in her manner to indicate depression – rather the opposite, insisted her sister – but she had developed a habit of walking alone, something she had done since her college days as a method of clearing her head. On the morning of her death she had been seen by several people walking towards her favourite spot along Whisker Hill and on to what was known locally as 'the forty steps'. These steps led down to the railway embankment where her body was later found, with her severed head on the lines a short distance from the last step. No signs of violence were found, nor had she been robbed. Signalman Henry Boddy, the last person to see her alive, watched her pass his signal box at 7.45 p.m.; within minutes she was dead, hit by the 7 p.m. train from Mansfield. Concerned about how the body lay when discovered but not convinced of suicide, the coroner sought a medical opinion with regard to her general health. But there was nothing to suggest any kind of mental decline or mental illness. The only salient fact came from her two sisters, who told the court that Louisa occasionally suffered fainting fits. This, the coroner decided, could be the only explanation for so baffling a death. Perhaps Louisa fainted at the trackside, her head striking the line as she fell, and had been decapitated by the train before she could regain her senses? He left the answer to that question open and returned a verdict of misadventure.

4 MAY   1882   William Bradburn was found wandering around the streets of Farndon, near Newark, a little after 8 a.m. dressed only in his shirt and trousers, and with blood streaming from a wound in his throat. Two men, who both knew Bradburn, ran to his assistance and took him back to his own house where they laid him on the kitchen floor. Dr Clelland Clarke, whose surgery was close by, was sent for and attended within minutes. Near neighbour Agnes Farnworth, who had entered the house with the doctor, was sent upstairs to see if there was a bed that he could be taken to. As she entered the only upstairs room in the house she discovered the bodies of Bradburn's stepdaughter and son, both lying on the house's only bed. The girl, 17-year-old Phoebe Hardy, lay on top of her stepbrother Peter, a boy of only nine. Both had had their throats cut, the boy's so severely that the head was almost severed. Dr Clarke's assessment was that both had died some

Retford's old courthouse.

hours earlier, the girl having been savagely beaten about the head before her throat was slashed open. When the police arrived they found the razor used in the killings lying discarded in a corner of the kitchen. On the kitchen table was a black envelope addressed to Bradburn's mother Elizabeth. The short letter it contained blamed the double murder on his stepdaughter Phoebe, citing her involvement with a man he had taken a particular dislike to as the motive. On a piece of slate left beside the note he had written that he had been suffering from fits and was not always aware of his own actions. Later investigations revealed he had threatened young Phoebe's life a few days earlier and that over the previous few weeks his mental state had declined considerably. Some fourteen years earlier he had been locked away in a mental asylum in Prestwich and had clearly never fully recovered. He was declared insane and sent to an asylum.

The Saracen's Head Inn, Southwell, where Charles I surrendered to the Scottish army at the end of the English Civil War.

1646 Famed for a King! Southwell received its most famous royal guest on this day after the battle of Naseby and so played its role in the tragic affairs of King Charles I. After years spent fighting a civil war to protect his crown, a beaten and much subdued Charles I fled Oxford and came to the Saracen's Head at Southwell, where he dined with his Scottish commissioners before surrendering himself to their uncertain security. He was right not to trust them: a year later they handed him over to Parliament.

5 MAY

6 MAY **1865 Strange death in Arnold** An inquest held at the Horse and Jockey public house in Arnold heard how 60-year-old framework knitter William Knight had been found lying face-down in the street just before midnight two days earlier. Known as an intemperate man, he was assumed to be drunk and was carried home by three friends. He died sitting in a chair an hour or so later. According to medical evidence his death had been caused not by alcohol abuse but as the result of a blow to the head. A number of witnesses told the court that there had been an altercation earlier in the evening between the dead man and James 'Jemmy' Foster, resulting in Knight being pushed to the floor, but no one could say if any blows had been struck. In the absence of evidence the case was closed and Knight's death was left unresolved.

7 MAY **1797** William Fletcher (aged 25), a private in the 46th Regiment of Foot, was one of a party on escort duty, travelling from Doncaster to the south of England with a prisoner who had been charged with desertion. After stopping at a pub at Newark the men were joined by George Willis, who expressed some knowledge of the army and Fletcher's regiment in particular. The two men struck up an easy friendship and spent much of the afternoon in each other's company away from the other soldiers. As evening arrived Fletcher, for some inexplicable reason, suddenly stood up and accused Willis of being a deserter like his prisoner. Willis remonstrated with him, insisting he was no such thing. Realising that he was never going to convince the young private, he left the pub. Pulling a pistol from his belt, Fletcher ran into the street after him and shot him once in the leg. Unable to stand, the unfortunate Willis lay on the ground and pleaded his innocence to the gathering crowd. Fletcher meanwhile calmly reloaded, walked across to where Willis lay and shot him dead.

8 MAY **1801** Michael Denman (aged 24), William Sykes (31) and William Ratcliffe were arrested after breaking into the Brown Cow public house at Mansfield and stealing £8 in banknotes. Denman and Sykes each had a criminal record stretching back into their early teens. From a young age they had been involved in a variety of petty thefts, had been caught poaching, had stolen fowls from neighbouring farms and had regularly broken the rules of the Sabbath. Their involvement in crime stepped up a level when they took part in a serious robbery at the Retford wine vaults in 1779, when some 16 gallons of gin was stolen. They robbed the Old Mill at Mansfield at around the same time and more recently had held up the Mansfield stagecoach at Eaton and stolen a box of new shoes and gloves. Ratcliffe in contrast had no serious criminal past. Offered his freedom in return for a full confession implicating the two old hands, he didn't hesitate. At their trial Denmand and Sykes were found guilty and sentenced to death, being executed together on 5 August.

9 MAY **1865 A Horse in a China Shop** A startled horse broke loose from a cart and in panic ran off down Derby Road. Realising what was about to happen, an alert constable succeeded in moving people out of its way as the frightened animal lunged at the plate-glass window of Green's Wines and Spirits shop. Fortuitously the owner's wife had just stooped down to retrieve an item from beneath the counter as the horse, showered in broken glass, leaped over her head, smashed every piece of glassware in the shop, and finally skidded to a halt 10ft from where she stood. The same policeman dragged her out through the broken window and both shopkeeper and horse survived unscathed, which is more than can be said for the shop's stock of fine wines.

1865   Henry Attenborough (aged 40) of Basford, Nottingham, stood in the dock at Nottingham's courthouse and pleaded not guilty to having raped 7-year-old Mary Ann Foulds. He had told police that he had never raped the little girl but had always paid her. 'He had given her 3 pence, sixpence, a shilling and a penny,' according to Police Constable Sansem. These amounts covered each of their meetings. The court sent him for trial at the autumn assizes.

1882   Baby Farming at Cropwell Bishop In the dock at Bingham's petty sessions, before Mr William Tidmas, Catherine Cook was charged under the baby-farming act of having received two babies under the age of one year for the purpose of nursing and maintaining them for money. According to Cropwell Bishop's Police Constable Coy, the house in which she lived had only one bedroom, yet there were four children sleeping in it, and over the past few years two babies had died while in her care – no doubt, he added, because of the dirty and unkempt conditions in which they lived. A search of the house had also revealed a quantity of laudanum, which, it was believed, had been used to keep the children quiet. Catherine denied that drugs were necessary to put the babies to sleep: 'The strong air of Cropwell Bishop caused the children to sleep naturally.' Laudanum, she told the bench, was only used to soothe sore fingers whenever they had been trodden upon. Found guilty, she was given the choice of 25s fine or six months' imprisonment. She paid the fine.

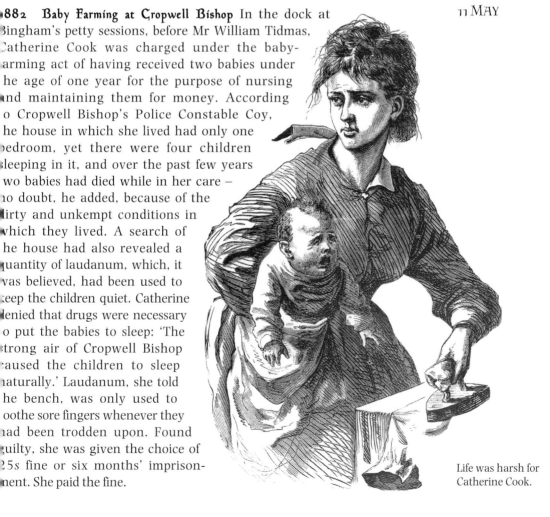

Life was harsh for Catherine Cook.

12 MAY **1865** The *Nottingham Journal* reported that Charles Becket, John Wilson and Robert Roberts had appeared at the Borough police court charged with burglary. They had been spotted a week earlier by an alert beat bobby trying to find a way into the premises of lace manufacturer William Hodson, and the police had mounted a watch. When the three unsuspecting burglars forced their way in the police simply waited for them to leave and arrested the three in possession of their spoils, 12lb of silk worth 46s per lb.

13 MAY **1882** Banjo player Samuel Dennis was brought before Newark magistrates after being found lying drunk on the pavement on Baldertongate completely covered in whitewash. He could offer no explanation for the whitewash, and having attempted to clean his coat, appeared in court wearing what looked like a black and white polka-dot jacket. He was ordered to be ejected from the town forthwith.

14 MAY **1870 Pickpocket Captured at Newark** Accomplished thief John Churchill (aged 46), alias Frederic Knowles (but also known under six other aliases), was arrested in Newark after being seen picking the pocket of Mary Ann Bailey at Newark station. He pleaded not guilty and very adroitly conducted his own defence, but after being convicted he admitted his guilt and asked for a further twenty similar robberies to be taken into account. He was sentenced to eighteen months' hard labour.

15 MAY **Old Punishments: The Newcastle Cloak** The Newcastle cloak consisted of a wooden barrel with an iron collar and chains. Any young woman who had 'misbehaved' would be partially stripped and put inside the 'wooden petticoat'. Her neck would be secured by the collar and her hands and feet chained to the barrel's sides. She would then be paraded through the village streets to be mocked by the usually hostile crowd.

Artist's impression of the Newcastle cloak.

16 MAY **1882** Militiamen Samuel Sharp and George Cullen were both charged at Newark District police court with desecration of the Sabbath by playing pitch and toss (flipping a coin and gambling

on whether if fell as heads or tails) on a towpath outside the town. Arrested by a plain-clothes policeman, they admitted their guilt and were fined 11s each.

1808 Daniel Lambert, possibly England's fattest man, arrived in Newark to exhibit himself to crowds who paid 1s each to see 'the heaviest man who ever lived'. Weighing in at over 50st Lambert never drank alcohol, ate only one course at any meal and was considered to be extremely strong. The former keeper of Leicester's house of correction, his weight gain had been caused not by overeating but by a medical problem. In order to ensure that he had sufficient money on which to live, he had decided some two years earlier to embark upon a series of tours around the country exhibiting himself as a curiosity. People flocked to see him. His body circumference exceeded 9ft, while each leg was more than 3ft round. At a time when the vast majority of people struggled just to feed themselves, and were consequently thin to the point of emaciation, one can perhaps understand his appeal. He died the following year while visiting Stamford races and was buried in a coffin measuring 4ft across at its widest point and made from some 112ft of elm wood.

17 MAY

1911 **The Mystery of Harry Daniels** Tommy to his friends, Daniels was a successful bookkeeper with a significant sum of money in his own bank account. He kept well-maintained and accurate company accounts and was described in court as being of a 'cheerful disposition'. He was discovered dead in a shed at the bottom of the gasworks yard near where he worked, his throat cut. No witnesses had seen him enter the shed, no one had seen any other person near by and there was no suicide note. At the inquest the coroner could find no reason to suggest he had killed himself and the police found no evidence of foul play. His death was left unresolved.

18 MAY

1892 The body of a 3-month-old baby boy was discovered in an ash pit at a farm near Newark. The baby had died some days earlier. Patrick Tuffy, a labourer, found the child's body but, thinking it was a dead lamb wrapped it up in an old skirt and threw it back into the pit. His work colleague, William Foster, alerted the police after Tuffy had told him of his find some hours later. Curious, Foster had examined the ash pit himself and instantly realised that the body was in fact a little baby. No one was ever arrested for the killing.

19 MAY

1770 John Lord was found guilty of stealing curtains from the Crown Inn, an extensive building that occupied a site on Long Row, Nottingham. He was sentenced to be publicly whipped from the Weekday Cross to the Malt Cross and then to the Hen Cross, before being released.

20 MAY

1801 On this day at 3 p.m. a terrific thunderstorm broke over Newark. Taking shelter beneath a large ash tree, Mary Kirk and a young woman named Ellen Bosworth, who had been working outdoors, were struck by lightning and killed instantly.

21 MAY

Nottingham's
Weekday Cross
as it looks today.

892   A smartly dressed man travelling by train through Newark suddenly **22 MAY**
decided that life was not worth living. Standing in the centre of the carriage
he was sharing with a group of women and another man, he calmly removed
a clasp knife from his pocket, opened out the blade and cut his own throat.
The women screamed and the man travelling with them made an attempt
to thwart the suicide, but they held him back fearing that if stopped the man
would turn the knife on them. As the train arrived at the station he opened
the carriage door and then fell dead on to the platform. Some £30 in notes,
£10 in gold and a silver watch was all he had on his person.

1767   Robert Downes, a travelling peddler, was arrested after a coroner's warrant **23 MAY**
had been issued against him for the murder of Thomas Greenwood, the 15-year-
old son of a Mansfield miller. Downes instantly confessed his guilt and apologised
for having killed the boy, but added in mitigation that he had been extremely angry
at the time and unaware of his actions. Greenwood had been one of a gang of
young lads who had shouted abuse at Downes, trying to goad him into some sort
of reaction. When that proved less than successful they gathered on street corners
calling him names, and then followed him around Mansfield until he gave chase.
All the boys managed to outrun him, except Greenwood. Born deaf and dumb,
he had some obvious difficulties, which meant he was often a step or so behind
his friends. Downes caught him and in a fit of anger stabbed him in the left side of
his chest, killing him instantly. As a result of his confession he was executed three
months later and was given the dubious honour of being the first man to be hung
in chains at Mansfield since 1642.

1681   On or around this date Elizabeth Longman, described as 'of middle **24 MAY**
years, thin visaged and about 40 years old', was publicly whipped in
Mansfield after being charged with begging. She was ordered to return home
to Kirton, along with her two children, within a period of two days or else
suffer a second whipping.

1892   The *Newark Advertiser* reported details of the inquest into the strange **25 MAY**
death of Thomas Roe. A 70-year-old retired farm bailiff, he had been
found with his throat cut lying on the bed at his home. According to police
evidence he appeared to have walked around the bedroom after cutting his
throat because quantities of blood had been found in different areas of the
room. Various items of clothing scattered around the room suggested he had
attempted to dress himself while bleeding from the self-inflicted wound in his
neck. No motive was offered to explain why he had killed himself, though the
evidence, according to the coroner, did seem to indicate that no one else had
been involved in his death. He speculated that Roe had changed his mind after
slashing himself with the razor – but it was far too late.

1780   Nottingham giant John Green died at the age of 70. Formerly a private **26 MAY**
in the army, he had lived much of his life in Narrow Marsh being easily
recognised by his 7ft frame wherever he went.

27 MAY

Old Punishments: The Thew A simple means of humiliation, the Thew consisted of a central wooden post around which was a small, narrow platform. The prisoner would be secured to this platform by an iron ring placed around their neck and their hands would be chained. They would then have to stand in full view of the watching crowd for the period of time set by the village parish (parish council).

28 MAY

Above: What was known as the Ossington Coffee Palace, Newark, *c.* 1915.

1803 Mrs Sarah Justice, a farmer's wife from Bole, Gainsborough, told a Nottingham court that Lowdham labourer William Hill had raped her earlier that year. Despite his strenuous denials he was found guilty and sentenced to death. But Hill was not about to go quietly. On the morning of his execution he refused to leave his cell and had to be dragged out to the courtyard. There he was placed in a cart, his hands chained to the sides, and carried off towards the place of execution. Released from the cart he immediately attempted to escape but was caught by the crowd and severely beaten with clubs before being dragged back to the waiting hangman. The following is and extract from a contemporary broadsheet:

Though you trifle with Patience, Kate, Margery or Joan,
Be warned by my fate, and let justice alone;
For sooner or later her vengeance each feels,
Her hands are of iron, though leaden her heels.

1812   Benjamin Renshaw, a framework knitter of Mansfield, was arrested after setting fire to a haystack and killing a ram. A man who had spent much of his life pursuing crime of one sort or another, he and his wife had lived for six years in the Mansfield poorhouse. He was already well known to the courts, so there was little chance of leniency when he finally appeared in the dock. Found guilty after one of his supposed accomplices turned King's evidence and betrayed him, he was executed in Nottingham from a cart. Sadly for him, within minutes of being launched into eternity, the rope slipped from his neck and rose up above his chin. The cart was brought back and the execution repeated. The body was then given up to his friends and interred at Mansfield.

29 MAY

1767   According to parish records an unnamed Long Eaton man was locked in the town gaol on this day after being arrested for the murder of his wife. After an earlier argument in the cowshed he had lost his temper and struck her across the head as she sat on a stool in Long Eaton Meadow doing the morning's milking. He then surrendered himself to town officials and expressed his regret and sorrow at his actions.

30 MAY

Theatre Royal, Nottingham, October 1904.

31 MAY **1826** Executed at Nottingham on this day were Joshua Shepherd (aged 25) and George Milne (34). According to broadsheets published at the time of the double hanging, Shepherd had been a criminal for much of his young life. Convicted of stealing a watch in 1816 when he was 15 years old, he had been convicted and sentenced to death at Nottingham's Assize Court. Only his age saved him from the gallows on that occasion, the sentence being reduced to six months in prison. Unfortunately, this had little impact on his behaviour. Imprisoned a second time within a year of release for assault, he was back behind bars after he broke all the windows of the Lion and Lamb public house. There was little doubt about the road he had chosen to follow. After robbing a shop in Bingham some months earlier, he had joined forces with Milne and two other men named Varley and Breedon to rob a drapery shop in Retford owned by Ann and John Wheat. It was an extremely successful business and therefore the premises were likely to be well stocked. After breaking in and stripping it out completely, they realised that the cart they had brought to carry the goods back to Nottingham was too small so after some debate they decided to hide a significant quantity in a tomb in Rampton churchyard and return for it on the following day. Unfortunately for the gang, four men with a cart moving around in the early hours of the morning were bound to arouse suspicion, and they did. They were all arrested as they entered Nottingham. What happened to Varley and Breedon is not recorded. Milne, it transpired, had deserted from the 4th Dragoon Guards after stealing all the silver from the officers' mess. He attempted to cheat the hangman by refusing to identify himself. It had absolutely no effect.

JUNE

To the Inhabitants of the Town of
NOTTINGHAM.

THE MAGISTRATES are very much concerned to obſerve the continuance of riot and depredation in this town : they therefore REPEAT their commands to all perſons *immediately to diſperſe to their ſeveral habitations :* And all maſters of families are ſtrictly charged to keep at home their reſpective apprentices and ſervants ——Should *this* Caution remain unattended to, and the peace of the town *not* be reſtored, the *moſt coercive and ſevere meaſures will*

IMMEDIATELY BE PURSUED
to enforce the preſervation of the public peace.

THE MAGISTRATES earneſtly entreat their Fellow-Townſmen to bear it impreſſed upon their minds, That the TOWN is dependent upon the COUNTRY for its ſupply of Bread corn—that unleſs peace and good order be reſtored, it is impoſſible for any exertions to induce the Farmers to ſend their corn to the town ; and, conſequently, thoſe who diſturb the public peace are the perſons who *really* and *truly* prevent the poſſibility of the friends of public tranquility from alleviating the ſufferings which they ſin-cerely deplore.

Exertions have been made, and are making, by the Magiſtrates, to BRING DOWN THE PRICE OF CORN—but without *internal* peace it will be impoſſible for that ſupply to enter the town which can alone produce a

REDUCTION OF THE PRICE
of Corn and Flour.

BY ORDER,
Geo. Coldham, *Town Clerk.*

Nottingham, 2d September, 1800.

(Burbage and Stretton, Printers, &c. Nottingham.)

Fig. 4 *Broadsheet regarding bread riots in Nottingham, 1800*

A 'do not riot' notice issued by
Nottingham Town and County.

1 June 1821 James Revel returned to Nottingham after serving fourteen years as a convict at Botany Bay. He published a verse account of his crime and conviction, and sold it successfully throughout Nottingham.

2 June 1771 A young domestic servant, Mary Jones, was walking back to Mansfield at around 10 p.m. after an evening out visiting friends when she was attacked by a man who attempted to drag her into nearby woodland. After a violent struggle she succeeded in beating him off, but not before he had robbed her of 9s. She later identified the man and he made a full confession. Unfortunately for Mary, the magistrate at the man's eventual trial forced her to drop the charges after the man made an offer to repay the money, promised to lead a better life and even offered to marry her.

3 June 1893 An inquest opened at Newark Hospital into the tragic death of 11-year-old John Cullen. He had been around horses for most of his short life and was killed just outside Balderton while driving a manure cart into town. As he reached down to grasp the reins they slipped to the ground; the horses panicked and began to gallop off and the young lad slipped between the horses' hindquarters and the cart. Both wheels ran over him, crushing him to death.

4 June 1893 At a little after 10 a.m. cries of 'Murder' were heard in Retford as Elizabeth White screamed for help before being thrown through a downstairs window. She and her husband Henry had been fighting since the previous night. Arriving home from the pub he had dragged her around the house by her hair, thrown her into the yard, beaten her and then allowed her back into the house but not into bed. Forced to sit up all night in the kitchen, by morning her anger had not subsided and when Henry walked downstairs for his breakfast she attacked him. Taking a poker, she broke every pane of glass in the downstairs windows, then ran outside, picked up a brick and hurled it at him. The brick missed but his fist struck home and her cries for help came just in time to save her life. Neighbours pulled Henry off just as he was about to strangle her. Unbelievably Retford magistrates fined him only 17s 6d.

1876   George Wyer was sentenced to three months' imprisonment after being found guilty of keeping an 'unlicensed asylum for profit and ill-treating a lunatic'. An army surgeon, Wyer had served throughout the Crimean War (1854–6). He had absolutely no knowledge of mental illness, for his experience, if not his true expertise, lay in surgery. Yet after settling in Newark, he had taken in his own half-sister after her family complained to him about her mental state. Charging the family a fee and promising to take care of her, he had then simply locked her away inside his own house and treated her abominably.   **5 June**

1865   William Dawbley had a reputation for unpredictable violence, particularly towards his wife Eliza, who had endured many years of brutal beatings from him that often resulted in his being sent to prison. However, despite all this she had remained a loyal, if somewhat wary, partner, and the two had continued to live together each time he was released. Regrettably for her she was to pay a heavy price for her misguided loyalty. Just five days earlier she had disturbed him as he cut his toenails with a penknife. The irrational Dawbley suddenly leapt at her in a frenzied attempt to cut her throat. Despite instinctively raising her arms to protect herself she suffered horrific injuries. Neighbours forced their way into the house after hearing her desperate screams for help and prevented him from murdering her. However, the court, despite Dawbley's violent history, sentenced him to only six months hard labour. What became of Eliza and William after his release on this occasion is not recorded.   **6 June**

1865   Thomas Whittaker left the bar of a Newark pub to visit the toilet in the back yard. As he returned he slipped from the top step of a flight of wooden steps and fell head first into a water butt. The landlord discovered him 10 minutes later after coming out of the pub to see where the man had gone. According to the inquest held this day he had drowned in 16in of water. The landlord was advised to put a lid on the 6ft water butt to prevent future accidents.   **7 June**

Old Punishments: Boiling to Death This barbaric punishment was introduced onto the statute books by Henry VIII in 1531 as a penalty for coining and poisoning. A fire was lit beneath a huge cauldron of water and as it reached boiling point the terrified victim would be plunged into it by means of a chain hung from a gantry. The body was subsequently lowered up and down until life was extinct.   **8 June**

1865   **Tragedy at Linby Village** The *Nottingham Journal* reported that on this day the coroner, Mr Swann, opened an inquest at the Horse and Groom public house into the discovery of the body of 16-year-old John Gothard, a needle-maker. He had gone swimming in the dam at Swift's Mill close to the village and had simply disappeared. After dragging the millpond his body was found some 60ft from the bank in 11ft of water.   **9 June**

10 June **1883** Two men sent underground at a Nottingham pit to attend to a sick pit pony were killed along with fourteen ponies after one of them carelessly lit a lamp and showed a naked flame. At the inquest the court was told that the men, being the first of the morning shift to go on to the coalface, had been instructed that under no circumstances were they to show any flame because the pit shaft was known to hold gas. The rescue team found one of the miners still alive; according to him his partner had refused to put the light out because he did not believe that gas had formed around the stable area. Unfortunately the man died before they could get him to the surface.

11 June **1801** West Bridgford farmer John Featherstone, having lost a number of cattle to thieves throughout the previous month, decided to set a trap for the rustlers. Setting guards at various locations around his land, he simply waited for what he believed would be an organised band to descend on his herd. Imagine his surprise when he discovered that the culprit was 11-year-old John Wright; he had managed to carry out all the thefts on his own, but was caught as he attempted to move a cow on to the Nottingham road. The court had scant regard for Wright's age, and after being found guilty at his trial he was sentenced to death. Fortunately for the young cattle rustler this sentence was commuted to a term in prison just before the execution was to have been carried out.

12 June **1765** In one of the most bizarre of customs William Wilson, a Nottingham breeches maker, was buried beside the main public highway because he had committed suicide by stabbing himself in the stomach. Before the body was covered over, a wooden stake was driven into the chest.

13 June **1786** On this day between 5 and 7 a.m. five prisoners successfully escaped from Nottingham's County Gaol. One used a stolen key while the other four broke through the ceiling of their cell, climbed out on to the roof and then let themselves down by means of a stolen length of rope.

Nottingham market, c. 1900. This postcard is addressed to a Master I. Wood, who had clearly been having a rather grim time – part of the message reads, 'I expect you have an abscess in the root of that tooth.'

1864   William Beals was tragically killed while grinding hot plates for the tops of kitchen ranges. The grinding stone, which weighed 22cwt, suddenly blew apart, killing Beals instantly and badly injuring a furnace man nearby.

14 JUNE

1876   An inquest held this day into the death of Sarah Lane at New Basford returned a verdict of wilful murder against her husband John. He was devastated by the crime he had committed, and was found later hanging from a tree near his home.

15 JUNE

1856   A strange death took place on this day at the Jolly Anglers public house, Plumptre Street, Nottingham. A baby was burnt to death as it lay on a bed in an upstairs room. No fire had been lit in the grate but a chest of drawers beside the bed was alight. After an exhaustive and detailed examination of the room and its furnishings, it was decided that the room immediately below had caused the fire. Heat had permeated through the chimney breast wall and been transferred to the chest of drawers which stood against it. This had ignited and the flames had then caught hold of the bedding. The inquest accepted the explanation and it was agreed that the baby's death had been accidental.

16 JUNE

1903   Two suicides were reported by the *Newark Advertiser*. Henry Stables, a widower, had walked into a barn and cut his own throat, while septuagenarian Daniel Jones had simply drowned himself in a pond at the bottom of his garden.

17 JUNE

1790   During the second day of riots in Nottingham a mob descended on the city and continued the violence that had begun twenty-four hours earlier. In a pitched battle in the market square on the second day of the riots a force of special constables was roundly beaten off and chased out into the surrounding streets. The crowd then smashed the windows of a number of buildings and succeeded in forcing an entry into

18 JUNE

An 1820 calendar for the Nottingham Assize Court detailing those prisoners whose trials were scheduled to be heard. (Nottingham Local Studies Library)

the bank. Sporadic musket fire broke out later from the bank's upper-floor windows, killing one unfortunate bystander and wounding several others. The army arrived towards the end of the afternoon and order was restored by midnight.

19 JUNE **1764** James Rutland was sentenced to death for burglary, but because he confessed the sentence was amended and he was ordered instead to be transported for life. But Rutland had no intention of being transported anywhere if he could help it. At a little after midnight he successfully broke out of his dungeon cell, sawed his way through a second door some 4in thick, and then attempted to break into the prison yard. His plan was to seize the well rope from the yard and then simply remove the bars from the kitchen window and lower himself down into Narrow Marsh. Unfortunately for Rutland he made too much noise in the attempt and was caught before he could break out into the yard.

20 JUNE **1690** After several days of freak weather conditions, exceptionally heavy rain brought the county to a complete standstill. Widespread flooding rendered most roads impassable. Much of the area around Newark was reported to be under water, with some parts of the town itself being cut off. In Nottingham the River Trent burst its banks and flooded large tracts of land across the eastern side of the county.

21 JUNE **1830** A reward of £10 was offered by Mr William Sharp to anyone who had information about the theft of an eel trunk containing 3st of eels.

22 JUNE **1840** At around this time Nottingham Workhouse housed more than 230 children, 70 of whom were under the age of five, along with their parents, and the routines of the house under which they all lived were made public. Breakfast, which was served after everyone had attended morning prayers performed by the governor at half past six in the morning, consisted of a bowl of porridge; men also received 7oz of bread and women 6oz. More bread was issued at suppertime. Throughout the week a strict menu of meals was adhered to.

Opposite: Southwell Workhouse today. Built in 1824 at a cost of £6,500 and known as Thurgarton Hundred Incorporated Workhouse, it served forty-nine parishes around Southwell. It was intended to house 158 paupers and was one of 600 similar institutions across England by the end of the Victorian era. Men were housed in the east wing, women in the west wing and children at the back.

Sunday:	7oz of beef and unlimited potatoes.
Monday:	Irish stew made from the bones of the meat used on the previous day with an additional quantity of meat.
Tuesday:	16oz of suet pudding.
Wednesday:	Broth, containing cooked carrots and various seasonal vegetables.
Thursday:	Meat, either beef or lamb, served in the same proportions as on Sunday.
Friday:	Pea soup in an unlimited quantity but with no bread.
Saturday:	Broth, the same as was served on Wednesday but this time with bread.

The menu makes interesting reading. The workhouse was a lifesaver for many people, described by James Orange (who originally published this information) as either destitute youth, worn-out age, shameless profligates, or those with wasting sickness, mental imbecility or bodily decrepitude.

1833 After an argument in Nottingham over a shotgun Richard Lowater grabbed hold of the stock and tried to wrest it from his friend's grasp. The friend, Richard Elliot, was not to be easily dispossessed and in the ensuing fight both men fell to the ground. The gun, which had earlier been loaded, went off and Elliot was killed. At his trial before Mr Justice Taunton, Lowater pleaded not guilty to murder and claimed the death had been accidental. The jury did not believe him and he was found guilty of manslaughter. The judge sentenced him to one year's imprisonment.

23 June

1793 Francis Walsh, a shoemaker with premises on Long-row, Nottingham, was accidentally killed on this day by his son. During the festivities to celebrate the king's birthday, the young man discharged a pistol extremely close to his father's shoulder. His intention, of course, was simply to startle him with the loud report. Regrettably the wadding used to load the pistol hit the man's neck and was so deeply embedded surgeons were unable to remove it. Walsh suffered intolerable agonies before dying in the early hours of the morning.

24 June

25 June   **1774**   John Parkin, a razor grinder, was robbed on this day of 7 guineas and 5 silver shillings at Sandy Lane, Arnold, as he made his way towards his home at Tideswell in Derbyshire.

26 June   **1783**   Riots broke out after a Nottingham hosier increased the prices of his hose by 2d; an effigy of the man involved was pinned to his door and his windows were smashed by bricks. The mayor read the riot act and a number of special constables were sworn in to restore order on the streets. They failed miserably, and only the arrival of a detachment of Horse Guards calmed the situation. But it was an uneasy peace and after the cavalry had left on the following day a mob attacked the mayor's house and fresh rioting broke out. This was eventually quelled by a force of 300 new constables armed with wooden staves.

27 June   **1865**   Election riots broke out in Nottingham when supporters of two rival candidates, Charles Paget and Samuel Morley, arrived at Nottingham station at a little after half past five in the afternoon. A stone-throwing crowd greeted their arrival and forced them to take shelter on the railway platform, where they successfully hid away from the rock barrage. But not for long: the stone-throwers soon burst through the railway gates. Within minutes the whole platform was set alight and running battles spilled out into the surrounding streets as the travellers ran for their lives. Serious damage was inflicted on almost all the business premises around the station area and it took police several hours to restore order. A significant number of men from both sides had been severely injured.

28 June   **1815**   News reached Nottingham that the Wollaton Prize-Fighter, known locally as Shaw the Life Guardsman, had been killed outside La Haye Sainte farm during the battle of Waterloo. During the farm's stout defence he sustained numerous wounds and died from loss of blood. Never beaten as a boxer, and a challenger for the title of Champion of England, his loss was mourned throughout the city. A monument to his memory and to two other Waterloo heroes was raised in 1877 on the anniversary of the battle and placed in the village of Cossall.

29 June   **1839**   John Driver (aged 26) made his final confession in his cell at Nottingham prison to the murder of Ann Hancock. He was born in Southwell but his family had moved to Caunton village near Newark some years earlier and Driver had worked on local farms as a general labourer. Ann Hancock had entered his life only briefly but with profound effect. Driver's father had fallen ill earlier in the year and the family had turned to Hancock, as the local grocer, for a remedy. It was common practice for grocers to sell miscellaneous items and drugs alongside the fruit and vegetables and Ann Hancock sold the family a bottle containing tincture of rhubarb, a well-known tonic. Unfortunately, after Driver's father had consumed a reasonable quantity his condition had worsened and only a few hours later he died. The examining

Waterloo memorial
in the grounds of
Cossall churchyard
to the memory of Life
Guardsman Shaw
and two of his fellow
officers.

surgeon realised instantly that this so-called tonic had in fact been laudanum. The Drivers had been given the wrong bottle. A later inquest exonerated Hancock from blame but the Driver family refused to forgive her. On 15 March John Driver broke into the little shop in the early hours of the morning, attacking Ann Hancock as she slept. He stuffed a piece of rag into her mouth and strangled her to death. Rather stupidly he then ransacked her house and stole everything he could lay his hands on, which was not a great deal. He was arrested within hours, and most of what he had taken was still in his trouser pockets.

30 June **1937** Walter Savill (aged 33) accidentally shot himself as he climbed over a fence carrying a loaded shotgun. He had left his home near Newark at about 8 p.m. intent on shooting a rabbit for his supper. He was found shortly afterwards having fired both barrels into his abdomen. Alive when he arrived at Newark Hospital, he survived long enough to see his wife but died a few hours later.

JULY

✝

Robert Pierrepont, Earl of Kingston and one of
Nottingham's wealthiest men. The Royalist was
killed on 24 July 1643 after being captured by
Cromwell's men at Gainsborough.

1 JULY **1918 Huge Explosion at Chilwell** At 8 p.m. the munitions factory at Chilwell was blown apart as 8 tons of high explosives went up killing 144 people and injuring some 250. The explosion was heard from as far away as the Vale of Belvoir, and the smoke could be seen from Bramcote. Most of the dead were so badly mutilated that their bodies could not be identified and so they were all buried together in a mass grave at Attenborough village. No explanation was ever found to account for the explosion. The Chilwell factory had played a crucial role in the war effort. According to published statistics 60 per cent of all the shells fired on the Western Front had been filled with explosive at Chilwell.

2 JULY **1829** Edward Revill (aged 60) was found guilty at Nottingham's Assize Court of shooting his neighbour, William Midhap, with intent to maim or kill. Fortunately the man survived. Revill on the other hand was sentenced to death, as were Peter Greasley (aged 21), who had shouted at Revill to fire, Edward's wife Sarah (57) and a woman named Ann Sporton (41), for aiding and abetting.

3 JULY **1825** An inquest at the Neptune Tavern in Meadow Platts heard evidence of murder against framework knitter Thomas Dewey. A married man, he had embarked upon an affair with Leicester woman Maria Austin two years earlier, and lived close to her lodgings in Nile Street, Nottingham. Maria, who was also married but was separated from her husband, had a child with Dewey in 1824 and at the time of her death was pregnant again with his second child. Dewey attacked her with a butcher's carving knife, stabbing her in her left side. This had caused her death, according to the coroner's court. The post-mortem examination had revealed that the point of the knife had penetrated her heart. Dewey's motive was jealousy. When Maria had originally left her husband and moved to Nottingham she had brought with her their only child. When this youngster became difficult to handle, possibly because of her pregnancy, she had travelled back to Leicester and brought her husband back to Nottingham. Fearing that she was about to return to her marriage, Dewey killed her in a jealous rage.

4 JULY **1853** Soldier Henry Ryder was sentenced to fifty lashes of the whip and two years' imprisonment after being found guilty of insubordination towards his superior officer, Colonel Shewel. After the first twenty-five lashes, inflicted in the square at Nottingham barracks, he was taken to hospital to recuperate before receiving the rest.

5 JULY **1775** Joseph Hatton was found guilty of attempting to pass a counterfeit shilling piece. The jury at his trial were told that a search of his house in Nottingham had revealed 235 circular pieces of metal, each about the size of a sixpence, 50 larger circular pieces possibly to be used as shillings, and a quantity of different types of chemical that when poured on to metal turned it a silver colour. He was sentenced to death.

1779 Nottingham labourer John Spencer was executed in front of a huge crowd of spectators after being found guilty of the double murder of Mary Yeadon and her son William, who both lived at the tollhouse near Scrooby. According to Spencer's confession, he had murdered them because he believed they had money on the premises. After walking to Scrooby and passing the time of day with them, he returned in the early hours of the morning and beat them both to death with a spiked hedge stake. All he succeeded in stealing from the house was a watch of no real value. After his trial at Nottingham's Assize Court the judge ordered that his body be hung in chains from a gibbet erected near the site of the murder. This wooden gibbet remained in place, complete with the decaying body, for sixty-seven years, finally collapsing in 1846.

6 JULY

1817 The body of 17-year-old Bessie Sheppard was discovered in a ditch alongside the Mansfield–Ravenshead road. She had been battered to death with a hedge stake that was found close to the body. The unfortunate Bessie had set out to walk to Mansfield in search of work as a domestic servant, wearing brand new shoes and carrying a brightly coloured cotton umbrella to keep the sun off her face. None of these distinctive items was found with her body, and when they did appear they quickly led to Bessie's killer. Charles Rotherham of Sheffield had attempted to sell them in the Three Crowns Inn at Redhill but could find no takers. He discarded the shoes, leaving them behind in the pub, and took the umbrella to Bunny, Nottingham, where he successfully sold it. But the shoes and the umbrella – the only items of value Bessie Sheppard had ever owned – were so distinctive that as the details of the murder surfaced so people remembered seeing Rotherham trying to sell them. He was eventually arrested in Loughborough and made a full and frank confession. At his trial the court was told that he had formerly served as a soldier in Wellington's peninsular army and had fought at the battles of Cuidad Rodrigo, Badajoz, Salamanca

7 JULY

Bessie Shepherd had dressed in her best clothes when she set out for Mansfield.

and Toulouse. But his previous good conduct made no difference to the jury's verdict. He was executed at Gallows Hill, Nottingham, on 28 July, and a group of Mansfield businessmen, moved by Bessie's tragic death, erected a stone memorial at the spot where her body was found. Many years later the widening of the A60 road led to the moving of this memorial, after which her ghost began to appear. It has been reported by a number of passing motorists.

8 JULY   **1692**   William Key was placed in the pillory at Newark between the hours of noon and 1 p.m. and upon his release was ordered to pay a fine of 10s. His offence was not recorded in the parish records.

9 JULY   **1792**   Chorister Thomas Bucklow, aged 9, was killed at Southwell Minster when he attempted to climb through a window on the south side of the choir.

Southwell Minster.

ext to the altar. Unfortunately for young Thomas the piece of oak timber he
ad grasped hold of was rotten. It gave way in his hand and he was killed as
is head hit the pavement.

693 On this day we find the only recorded instance of a person being
whipped from the tail of a cart. Frances Holmes, the mother of a bastard
hild, was ordered to be stripped to her waist and soundly whipped as she was
ragged from one end of Elton village, near Nottingham, to the other.

10 JULY

Whipping at the cart's
tail.

876   Fair science never taught to stray
        Far as the solar worlds or Milky Way.

11 JULY

etford eccentric John Clifton, for whom these lines were penned, died after
lifetime of studying the stars, making telescopes and creating what were
ermed electrifying machines. He also left behind a deadly legacy. He had
ong been fascinated by fireworks and throughout his life, whenever time
llowed, he had manufactured a variety of types to entertain both himself and

his friends. Regrettably for his sister, who had never exhibited any interest i his pyrotechnics, the component parts that combined to create the colourfu bangs she had often witnessed were a complete mystery. Sorting throug her late brother's personal belongings she discovered a tin canteen full o black powder, which she thought was of no importance or value. Advise by a servant to bury it in the garden, she decided the effort was too great an simply emptied the contents on to her fire. The resulting explosion blew out a the windows, threw the door off its hinges, completely demolished the house outer wall and killed her outright.

12 JULY   1870   Newark labourer George Paterson travelled by train to London an then made the short journey to Charing Cross Bridge, from which he jumpe to his death. He had claimed that he had been followed by the devil and deat was the only way to escape.

13 JULY   1884   The *Newark Advertiser* reported the discovery of the body of a youn man, named only as Cooke, on the railway lines on the outskirts of Newark He had been respectably dressed and the inquest decided that he had probabl fallen asleep beside the railway line after walking back from the arm barracks at Lincoln where he had attempted to enlist. Defective eyesight ha kept him out of the army and he had probably had too much to drink, whic had caused him to fall asleep. A passing train had struck him, causing severe blow to the head and killing him instantly.

14 JULY   1834   William Hinkley (aged 31) stood in the dock before the Hon. Si William Elias Taunton and in a faint voice pleaded not guilty to the murde of his wife Fanny four weeks earlier. Both had been born in Derby, where the had set up their marital home six years earlier. Fanny had fled from the hous in 1830 after a particularly brutal beating and taken lodgings in Nottinghar above a butcher's shop. She obtained work as the butcher's shop assistan and gained brief celebrity through her invention of a meat spread known a Polony. Unfortunately for Fanny her good fortune did not last and she wa forced to leave her lodgings when the butcher moved into the premises wit his new wife. Taking lodgings above Thomas Peck's confectioner's shop o Beck Lane, Nottingham, she turned her hand to other shop work and soo embarked on a relationship with a man named Bull. The two began to liv together, and the Peck family believed they were extremely happy. In Jun 1834 it all changed. After some diligent detective work William tracked he down and after a heated argument attacked her in her rooms with a knif Alerted by her frantic screams for help, landlord Thomas Peck forced his wa through the door. Fanny lay on the floor desperately trying to fight off he husband. Peck wrestled him away from her badly cut and bleeding body, bu not before William had cut her throat and killed her. Poor Fanny had suffere numerous stab wounds to her head, arms, hands, breasts and neck; she ha never stood a chance. Fortunately neither did William. He was sentenced t death for her murder and executed seven days later.

799 Blind James Brodie (aged 23), a native of Dublin, was executed for he brutal murder of a young boy named Robert Henesal (aged 8), who had cted as his eyes and as his guide. Blind since the age of 3, Brodie had taken o the roads as soon as he was able and travelled around Nottinghamshire s a beggar. Earlier in the year he had struck a bargain with an unnamed eeds woman for the loan of her son in return for 1s a week. Desperate for noney the woman had agreed. Her son was not even consulted and had no hoice but to become Brodie's guide. Terrified of him from the outset, Robert ndured numerous beatings in the few short months they were together, but ither through fear or simply because he had nowhere else to go, he stayed vith him. Had Brodie continued to make the payments to Robert's mother o one would ever have sought him out, but when the payments stopped the oy's mother demanded that the authorities find and return her son. A blind nan in Nottingham was not too difficult to locate, particularly one working s a beggar, but when Brodie was found he was alone. After questioning, rodie eventually confessed to having murdered the boy and led police to his rave in Sherwood Forest. Poor Robert had been beaten to death and horribly nutilated before his body was cast aside and covered over with leaves and ubbish.

15 JULY

646 Labourer, Richard Thornton was killed by falling masonry as he ssisted in the demolition of Newark Castle, which Cromwell had ordered to e destroyed after its surrender to Parliamentary forces. The intention was to nsure the castle could never be used as a fortress again.

16 JULY

The ruins of Newark Castle.

17 JULY   **1906**   The trial of Edward Glynn opened at Nottingham on this day. Indicte
for the murder of Jane ('Jenny') Gamble on Canal Street in Nottingham, h
had pleaded not guilty. Unfortunately for Glynn, at the time of the attack sh
had been walking along the street in conversation with a man named Henr
Gibson. Although the night was particularly dark, Gibson had recognise
Glynn and had chased after him as Jane lay dying on the pavement. H
failed to catch him but his eyewitness account of exactly what had happene

A calendar of
prisoners ordered to
take their trials at the
17 July 1823 Assize
Court. (Nottingham
Local Studies Library)

hat night was enough to secure a conviction. Glynn, who insisted that he had been drinking in Bulwell on the night of the murder, finally made a full confession shortly before his execution three weeks later, citing jealousy as his motive. The two had lived together as man and wife for some time before he left him to live alone and Glynn, believing she had begun an affair, had resolved to kill her.

1638   For committing perjury John Kitchen was ordered to be placed in Mansfield's pillory for two hours and to have both his ears fastened to the pillory with nails.   18 JULY

1830   Alexander Pritchard and Peter Stubbins (both aged 18) were arrested shortly after they had committed a highway robbery on the outskirts of Edwinstow. After lying in wait beside the Nottingham road they had stopped villager Henry Kemp and robbed him of 5s 2d. At their trial a week later Pritchard was sentenced to six months' imprisonment and a whipping, while his partner in crime received only a four-month sentence.   19 JULY

1823   John Freeman (aged 19) was sentenced to seven years' transportation after being found guilty of stealing six silver spoons from a house in Farnsfield.   20 JULY

1831   Found guilty of the rape of Mary Ann Lord on waste ground behind the Lord Rancliffe public house in Nottingham in April, William Reynolds (aged 18) and William Marshall (21) were both told by the judge, Sir Nicholas Conyngham Tindal, that neither deserved to live and that the city would be better placed without them. He then sentenced them both to death.   21 JULY

1866   Jane Revill (aged 18) was found guilty of the murder of her infant son shortly after his birth in May, and was sentenced to death. Fortunately for her the sentence was commuted to life imprisonment shortly before her execution.   22 JULY

1896   At Nottingham's Shire Hall John Rose appeared in the dock before Mr Justice Grantham and pleaded not guilty to the murder of his wife Mary. He had been unemployed since November 1895 and it was claimed in court that the two of them had argued violently on the night of 11 February after John discovered that Mary had spent the rent money on drink. The following day both were found lying on the bedroom floor with their throats cut. Mary was dead but John Rose was still alive though badly wounded. In court he insisted that Mary had instigated the attack and that he had fought her off. Mary was a well-built woman, so the argument had some credibility. Unfortunately for John, medical evidence suggested that her fatal wound had been delivered from behind – and as there were only two people in the bedroom on the night in question, he must have killed her and then attempted to commit suicide. The jury accepted the prosecution's version of events and John was found guilty. He was executed on 11 August.   23 JULY

The gated entrance
to Nottingham Shire
Hall's courtyard.

1643 One of Nottingham's wealthiest and most influential men, the Royalist   24 JULY
Robert Pierrepont, Earl of Kingston, was killed on this day. He and his men
were caught unawares by a large force commanded by Lord Willoughby
of Parham; they retreated but were eventually surrounded and captured
by Parliamentary forces at Gainsborough. Taken prisoner, Pierrepont
was sent off down the River Trent toward Hull in a small boat. However,
another Royalist force under the leadership of the Earl of Newcastle, whose
brother had died in Pierrepont's last skirmish, spotted the boat, which was
flying no flag of identification, and ordered it to pull into the bank. When
no acknowledgement was received they began to turn their cannon on it.
Realising what was about to happen, Pierrepont ran on to the deck in an
attempt to stop the firing but was hit by the first cannon shot, the ball cleanly
severing his body in half.

1773 Collier James Wollaton was convicted at Nottingham Quarter Sessions   25 JULY
of having attempted to blackmail farmer William Bingham by threatening
to inform all his friends in Mansfield that he had committed buggery with
a cow. He was ordered to be set in Mansfield's pillory at noon upon this day
and to remain there for one hour. The large crowd that gathered to watch
his humiliation peppered him with rotten eggs, dirt and sludge. After his
release he was returned to Nottingham's gaol to begin a twelve-month prison
sentence.

1777 In a freak accident 6-year-old Mary Allin fell from the rocks above   26 JULY
Stockwell Gate, Mansfield, landing on the cart track below just as a farm cart
was passing laden with goods for the town market. The driver had no time to
stop his horses and the little girl was crushed beneath the wheels.

1916 During the night German Zeppelin *L.13* attacked Newark. In the   27 JULY
darkness the airship veered off course and all its bombs fell on the outlying
villages. No casualties were reported but some damage was caused to property
and a number of windows were broken by the explosions.

1837 The trial opened at Nottingham of Thomas Greensmith, who was   28 JULY
accused of the murder of his four children, John (9), William (7), Ann (5)
and Mark (2) in their Basford home. There was never any real doubt as to his
guilt. After an argument with his landlord over rent arrears, during which
Greensmith had been threatened with eviction, he had strangled each child
in turn as they slept. At the inquest held at the Fox and Hounds public house
in Basford on the day after the bodies were discovered, he had freely admitted
his guilt to the coroner. According to his own testimony, fear of losing his
home had forced him to kill the children, otherwise, he believed, they would
have been taken away from him. To trial judge the Hon. Sir James Allan Park,
the question was one of sanity. Was Greensmith insane or did he know what
he was doing? Had he not sold his children's shoes on the morning after the
murders, the jury would perhaps have accepted a plea of insanity. But once

it was shown that he had profited from their deaths he had no chance. Found guilty, he was executed in August.

29 JULY 1766 Footpads William Wainer and James Bromage stood among the congregation at St Mary's Church, Nottingham, and listened to the vicar give a sermon relating their crimes. Afterwards they walked the short distance to the graves that had been dug for them, each lying down in his own grave to check it was a perfect fit. The following day both were executed before a large crowd.

30 JULY 1830 Edward Vobill (aged 19) and Richard Fearn (18) stood in the dock to hear the judge tell them that Nottingham would benefit by not having them living anywhere near it. Found guilty of stealing a pocketknife, a pair of pincers and various other items from the Sneinton shop of Thomas Marshall, they were sentenced to be transported to Australia for life. No doubt Nottingham breathed a sigh of relief!

31 JULY 1828 George Dickenson (aged 22) could never have imagined that when he stopped Retford labourer George Merrils in the street and robbed him of his pocketbook, he too would make the long journey to the Australian continent. But at his trial the judge ordered him to be transported for life.

AUGUST

Chain Lane, Newark. The old town cells lay to the right of
this lane behind the shops in the Buttermarket.

1 AUGUST   1828   On this day 21-year-old John Shipley, who had a record for petty theft, was sentenced to death for stealing a hog sheep from Mansfield farmer John Fox.

2 AUGUST   1828   John Lowe (aged 21) and his good friend Henry Hill (23) were found guilty of 'sacrilegiously and burglariously breaking and entering the parish church at Winthorpe and stealing therein 3 cushions'. It was by any standards a petty crime and doubtless neither benefited from it – especially when the judge at their trial declared that they were to be executed at Nottingham.

3 AUGUST   1809   On this day 34-year-old Thomas Lampin was executed for having forged a bill of exchange for £100 with the intent to defraud Newark gentleman Peter Selby. He had no criminal history and such a fraud seemed at odds with his character. In court, however, it became apparent that he had committed the crime because of a downturn in his business and he needed to raise £100 to clear his debts. It had always been his intention to pay this money back to the lending bank before Selby discovered the theft. Unfortunately, it had been the chance discovery of his botched forgery and not the theft that had brought him to court, and the judge showed no mercy.

4 AUGUST   1885   **The Trumpet Street Murder** James Tucker was executed in the yard of Nottingham's St John's Street Gaol for the appalling murder of his lover Elizabeth Williamson, whom he had burnt to death in the front room of his lodgings. Tucker showed no remorse. A violent drunkard, he had lived with Elizabeth for nine years in various houses around Sneinton; in March 1885 they moved to a house in Trumpet Street, Nottingham. By this time their relationship had degenerated to such an extent that fierce arguments were commonplace. Tucker's apparent hatred for his partner seemed to be reciprocated by Elizabeth, who would purposely goad him, trying almost perversely to elicit some kind of reaction. But she could never have envisaged the violent rage that possessed him on 9 May. After an evening in the nearby Horse and Trumpet public house they began fighting almost as soon as they got home. Tucker knocked Elizabeth to the floor and repeatedly kicked her, and then threw paraffin from a stone jar over her prone body, struck a match and dropped it onto her skirts. By the time neighbour Henry Emerson forced his way into the house she was completely alight but still being viciously attacked as she writhed in agony on the kitchen floor. Emerson knocked Tucker over and doused the flames, but poor Elizabeth died six days later. Unfortunately for Tucker, though, she managed to make a death-bed deposition detailing her version of the night's events to the police. This convicted Tucker at his trial. There could be no defence for the awful murder he had committed.

5 AUGUST   1824   Charles Colclough (aged 23) and Thomas Hall (20) were found guilty of attacking Charles Benjamin on the outskirts of Nottingham and stealing from him a handkerchief valued at 5s 6d. They were sentenced to be transported for life.

1829   Just why William Wood (aged 28) broke into a house at Mansfield and stole 38lb of horsehair was not explained in court. But for the young Mr Wood it proved a crime too far. Found guilty of a number of other robberies and housebreakings he was sentenced to death.

1828   At the same Assize Court hearings brothers Thomas (aged 42) and Joseph Hallam (48) admitted they had stolen a 'fat wether [wedder] sheep' from Costock farmer George Woodruff with the intention of slaughtering it for food. Both were sentenced to death.

1751   The life and times of Nottingham's most famous adventurer, Captain John Deane, were recounted in a Nottingham courtroom on this day. Born in 1679, Deane had run away to sea to escape prosecution for poaching, eventually achieving the rank of captain. He left the navy in 1710 and went into business with his brother; they bought a ship, filled it with valuable merchandise and Deane sailed it to America. Unfortunately the vessel was wrecked on the New England coast, and Deane and the crew had to endure twenty-six days without clothing or food. The survivors were forced to resort to cannibalism before they were rescued in January 1711. Deane finally arrived back in Nottingham. Promptly recruited by the government as a spy, he was sent off to Russia where he stayed for some years, finally retiring to his native city. None of this mattered a jot to Joseph Milner, who had robbed Deane on the highway, but it did to Mr Justice Wright, who took an exceedingly dim view of young men attacking aged heroes. Milner, along with fellow robber John Smith, was sentenced to death.

1844   Twelve people were crushed to death as the jeering crowd that had turned out to see William Saville 'turned off' suddenly swayed towards the scaffold as the executioner released the trap. Those caught at the front had nowhere to go and were simply trampled underfoot as those behind them tried to stay on their feet. There was no such problem for one of Nottingham's most infamous murderers. Saville had few friends left after he was found guilty of the murders of his wife Ann and their three young children back in May. All had been found lying in the grass near woodland at Colwick with their throats cut. The trial had caused a sensation, particularly as much of it was reported by the *Nottingham Journal* in detail. The huge crowds that had come to watch the execution had done so because they wanted to see the monster hanged, such was the sense of revulsion felt by many who had read the lurid accounts. Saville declined the opportunity to address this noisy multitude because he felt they would have jeered and barracked him. No doubt he was right. Had he done so, it is quite possible that many more would have died in the crush around the scaffold.

Overleaf: Broadsheet of 1844 detailing the trial of and murders committed by William Saville.

1899   Over a thousand people gathered outside Nottingham's Bagthorpe prison waiting for the clock to strike eight. As it did so they fell silent, aware

Some Particulars

OF THE

LIFE, TRIAL,

BEHAVIOUR,

AND

EXECUTION

OF

WILLIAM SAVILLE,

AGED TWENTY-NINE YEARS,

Who was hanged in Front of the County Hall, Nottingham, on Wednesday, August 7, 1844,

FOR

MURDERING HIS WIFE AND THREE CHILDREN.

"THOU SHALT NOT KILL," was one of the commandments transmitted by the Almighty to Moses, for the governance of the children of Israel; and the penalty for the infraction of that law was conveyed in the terms, "*He that smiteth a man, so that he die, shall surely be put to death.*" The law has since been acted upon by all nations of men; and not only to those who committed murder was the punishment of death awarded, but at times men were put to death for the most trivial offences. Happily the criminal code of this country has recently undergone a revision, and it is now likely that we shall never more see so disgusting an exhibition as the deliberate destruction of a fellow creature in public, except for murder. It would be well even in cases of this nature also, if punishment of death were abrogated, and other punishment substituted, as men ought not, in the present day, to be actuated by principles of revenge: our laws inculcate this spirit. Besides, the lives of those individuals who commit capital crimes, generally show that the state is responsible for having created a predisposition to crime, by having neglected to provide intellectual culture for those who are left to their own blind guidance through life, without receiving any aid to virtue in the shape of instruction. These remarks may receive some illustration by observing the particulars of the history of the murderer, who has this day suffered death for destroying his wife and three children.

The life of William Saville shows a strange and varied picture of the manner in which the children of the lower classes are frequently left to struggle for an existence. Saville's father, who died about two years since, was a native of Bidworth, and at the time of William's birth, resided at Arnold, where he obtained a living by stocking-making; he was a man of very irregular habits, and cared little for the comfort of his wife, or the education of his children. Some years before, he had been in the army, where he had acquired habits of dissipation, which unfortunately he continued to practise through life. The maiden name of his mother was Terry, daughter of a Mr. Richard Terry, who formerly lived at the upper end of the village of Arnold; she is said to have been in all respects the reverse of her husband—careful, kind, and virtuous—and, had she lived a few years longer, it is more than probable that virtues might have given a different tone to the mind of the subject of this narrative; unfortunately, however, she died when he was only two years old. The father became a confirmed drunkard, and his children were frequently left to starve, or to subsist on the charity of neighbours, whilst he was drinking. It was no uncommon thing for him to take his work in on a Saturday, at Nottingham, and not to return to Arnold until the middle of the following week, after he had spent his earnings in drunkenness and debauchery. The consequence of this is obvious: the poor motherless children, left to shift for themselves, endured misery too shocking to describe. To this early neglect, the selfishness displayed by William Saville in after life, may fairly be attributed. When old enough, the subsequent murderer hired himself to a farmer, at Bidworth, as an agricultural servant; and in this employment he continued for some time, with various masters, until about fourteen years since, when his father learnt him the art of stocking-making. During his youth, his conduct was far from praiseworthy; how should it be otherwise, when he had been actually cradled in ignorance and vice? When Saville was about twenty-one years of age, he resided at the house of an individual named Lynch, at Arnold; here he became acquainted with the young woman who was afterwards his wife, and for murdering whom and her children he has suffered the penalty of death. The young woman's name was Ann Ward, a native of Lincolnshire; she had been in the service of Mr. Buchan, late of the High-pavement, Nottingham, for nine years. Whilst in the service of Mr. Buchan, she became acquainted with a young man of Daybrook, by whom she had a child. That child was placed with Mrs. Lynch, to nurse, and by going over to Arnold, on a Sunday, to see it, the acquaintance with Saville was made. This acquaintance afterwards led to marriage. The conduct of Saville, as a husband, never showed that he was fond of his wife, as he always treated her unkindly: and as a father also his conduct was brutal. The friends of his wife frequently did much for him, but he spent whatever he obtained, and soon was as badly off as ever. During the period of his marriage, he underwent many vicissitudes; he was tried at the November sessions, 1837, for felony, and sentenced to three months' imprisonment; and on the 26th of November, 1841, he was committed to prison for two months, for leaving his wife and family chargeable to the parish. A day or two before Christmas last he again neglected them, and they went into the workhouse, on the 2d of January. Saville then obtained employment with Mr. Robert Sutton, Birch-row, Radford, with whom he continued till the period of his apprehension for the murders. Soon after he went to reside with Mr. Sutton, Saville contracted an acquaintance with a young woman, whom he frequently asked to marry him. Previous to this time he had represented himself as an unmarried man, and never would acknowledge that he had children until he was obliged to it. The wife of Saville, with her children, came out of the workhouse on Monday, the 20th of May last, and proceeded to the house of a friend named Wardle, residing in Wood-street. Mr. Wardle went with her the same day to Mr. Sutton's, to seek her husband. He was not in, but they afterwards met him at the Pelican public house. The oldest little girl

stay with them. After a few minutes' conversation, Wardle left them together, and returned to his work. The woman and her children, in the course of the same afternoon, took up their lodging till the next morning at Wardle's house, and she said that her husband was to fetch them the next morning, and that he meant to take them to a relation's house at Carlton. Upon coming out of the workhouse, Mrs. Brownsword, Mrs. Saville's sister, had given her five shillings and sixpence, two ounces of mixed tea, and half a pound of coarse raw sugar. On the next morning (Tuesday), Saville went into Wood-street, at nine o'clock, to fetch her in bed, but waited till she got up, and then had a walk, but returned about ten o'clock. During Saville's absence, the unfortunate woman said to Mrs. Wardle, "As long as we have been married, I never knew he had any relations at Carlton." They all went away together, he carrying the little boy, and the mother leading the two little girls.

A little after one o'clock, on the same day, Saville returned to Wardle's house, and asked whether his wife had returned. He appeared to be much out of breath, and pretended to be very anxious to know where his wife and family were. The tale he told was, that he had accompanied them in the morning to the top of the street, and that then his wife had turned "very nasty," and she left her. His dress appeared to Mrs. Wardle to be the same as it had been in the morning. The same evening, between eight and nine o'clock, Saville again went to Wardle's house, and said he was afraid his wife had destroyed the children and then herself. Mrs. Wardle replied, "No, Mr. Saville, she has not made away with herself and children. What have you done with them?" He then began to cry aloud, and said, "Oh, my children, my children." Saville went away saying he would go somewhere else to seek for them. The next day he went again to Wardle's, and Mrs. Wardle sent for a policeman, and had him taken into custody. This was said to be done more for his safety than anything else, as a mob of people were threatening him.

On the next day (Wednesday), he was taken to the Police Office, where he underwent a long examination, in which he told the magistrates the same tale he had told Mrs. Wardle, besides many other fabrications. Upon his person were found a quantity of mixed tea, in a wrapper similar to that which Mrs. Saville was seen to put into her pocket the previous morning, and some money. [He had been heard to say, on the morning, that he had spent all his earnings.] When his clothes were examined, it was found that there were a few spots of blood on the right leg of his trousers, and the knee of his left leg appeared to have been discoloured by kneeling on clay and grass. During his examination at the Police Office, a messenger arrived, stating that the bodies of a woman and three murdered children had been found at Colwick!

On Friday, the 24th of May, an inquest was commenced at Colwick. A number of witnesses swore to having seen the prisoner and his family in different parts of the road to Colwick; he was traced from Wood-street to within a few yards of the spot where the bodies were found, and was seen coming away without them! John Swinscoe, of Carlton, discovered the bodies of the three children; he approached them slowly, thinking they were asleep, but upon getting close to them, he exclaimed to his son, who was a few yards off. "Oh! Abraham, Abraham, what a shocking sight I have seen." His son fetched the constable of Colwick, and then the body of the woman was discovered behind an alder bush, at four yards' distance. There was a continuous track between the place where the woman lay and the spot where the children were found, caused by the woman having been dragged on her back. In her left hand, which was free from blood, was a bloody razor. The inquiry continued the whole of Friday, and during a portion of Monday and Tuesday, when the jury returned a verdict of "Wilful murder" against Saville, and he was committed for trial at the next assizes. He was tried on Saturday, the 27th of July, before Lord Chief Justice Denman, when a strong chain of circumstantial evidence was established—two witnesses swore to a conversation at the police office, containing Saville's confession to the murders, before the bodies were found!—and the medical evidence showed it was impossible for the woman to have done it herself. The jury returned a verdict of "Guilty." During the trial, the prisoner was quite unmoved, although very attentive. His Lordship, in passing sentence, feelingly exhorted him to prepare for death, and told him that it would be in vain to hope for mercy.

After his condemnation, Saville's mind underwent a considerable change. For the first four or five days, he strove to act like a stoic; he did not seem to fear death, but spoke of his determination to meet it "manfully." On Friday night, however, he suffered much from troublesome dreams, and on Saturday his stubborn mind was thoroughly broken: he cried like a child, and lamented his condition aloud. He was much easier on Sunday morning, in consequence of having made a full confession to the chaplain on the previous evening. Since then he has been careful and inquiring, eagerly listening to anything calculated to give him hope of the pardon of God. This morning early, he prepared himself with confidence, and at eight minutes past eight o'clock he was plunged into eternity by the hand of the hangman.

The rush of the crowd, when the drop fell, was terrific. Many were seriously injured, and a number of persons are killed.

R. SUTTON, PRINTER, BRIDLESMITH-GATE, NOTTINGHAM.

hat before the chimes had finished Elias Torr had been executed inside the rison compound. He had been found guilty of the murder of his daughter Mary Ann in a moment of sheer madness. The murder had taken place at Hickling Pastures on the Nottingham–Melton Mowbray road after a heated rgument during which Elias had accused his wife of infidelity. With her oungest daughter Ruth and 27-year-old Mary Ann, she had fled the house nd run towards the neighbouring house of William Doleman. He gave her anctuary but was unable to prevent Elias smashing through the front door nd firing the single shot that killed Mary Ann. Full of remorse, Elias never hid rom his guilt but insisted that he had fired accidentally.

767   The body of Robert Downes was hung in chains from a gibbet at the orner of Lichfield Lane End, Mansfield, near a place known locally as the ravel pits. Described by the *Nottingham Journal* 'a silly fellow, nearly an idiot', Downes, who had spent most of his fifty-two years travelling between Derby nd Nottingham as a peddler, had confessed to the murder of 15-year-old Thomas Greenwood and to a significant number of robberies and thefts.

821   Two women who had turned to highway robbery appeared before Nottingham magistrates on this day. Ann Spencer (aged 19) and Catherine O'Brien (16) were found guilty of robbing Robert Faulkes of his purse ontaining 12s. Spencer, who already had a criminal past, was transported or fourteen years while O'Brien received the lesser sentence of eighteen months' hard labour.

824   William Pratt (aged 23) lived up to his surname when he stole a coat rom a neighbour. The court sentenced him to be whipped within the grounds f Nottingham's prison.

839   Chartist riots broke out across Mansfield on this day and the local eomanry, called out to restore order, were driven out of the market square y a hail of stones. Only the arrival of a troop of cavalry late in the afternoon uelled the riot after they had formed up and charged into the crowd with rawn sabres. Prior to 1832 the only people that held the right to vote in lections were those holding property, a total of 435,000 voters. The working ublic demanded reform and in 1832 Lord Grey forced through a Reform Act hat increased the electorate by some 200,000, but the principle of owning roperty remained unchanged. Those denied the vote, most of the country's workforce, drew up a list of demands known as the People's Charter. This made six demands: annual general elections, secret ballots, votes for all men, ayment of MPs, abolition of the property qualification for MPs, equal-sized onstituencies. For the next ten years those that supported this list were nown as Chartists.

773   Rioting broke out in Mansfield after a prize-fight between Mansfield hampion boxer Bandox and a Nottingham contender was brought to a

The
DYING SPEECH,
CONFESSION,

AND
WORDS
OF

JOHN MILLER,

Who was Executed on Nottingham Gallows, on Wednesday
August 16th, 1797.

For COW STEALING.

JOHN MILLER, the unfortunate subject of this narrative, was committed on July 8th, by the Honourable Henry Sedley, charged on the oaths of John Vessey, William Thomson, and Samuel Hickton, with stealing, taking and driving away, Three Cows, the property of the said John Vessey;—he was born at Eckering in this county, of industrious parents, who gave him but a slender education, a circumstance much to be regretted, as ignorance is too frequently the parent of vice; another circumstance which adds to the misfortune of his weak education is, his being brought up to no regular business, being a labourer from his youth, and naturally of a loose disposition, which exposed him much to the vices that persons without a Calling are frequently subject to; when he grew up for a while he followed the practice of buying rabbit skins and a number of other articles; his first robbery at an early age, was the stealing a Cow from his own Father, and when told of it he hoped the offender might soon be brought to justice, after which he was an accomplice with some others in a variety of robberies, he stole three Cows, two of which he sold at Newark, and one at some other place near there, for this theft he was apprehended, and had the good fortune to be discharged without punishment, for want of sufficient evidence, but such was the foulness of his nature, and the hardness of his heart, so blind was he to his best interest, that he would not profit by this favourable circumstance, but, "like the dog to his vomit," re-took to his former evil courses. He was concerned in stealing a Horse from a Mr. Capps at Barlow, near Newark, which was sold at Thorney in Lincolnshire, to a Butcher of Hull; also stole a Mare of Mr. Belfields of Farnton, near Newark, sold her to a man whose name he does not know, four miles from Spilsbury; was concerned in the stealing a Horse from a Gentleman in this town, and a from a Farmer near Bridgford, when he has been in fear of being taken, (such is our information) that he has been known to kill stolen horses, to boil them for their fat, and sell their hides; it was his constant habit to steal horses in Lincolnshire and neighbouring Counties, and take them up the country to Derby, Litchfield, and the fairs that way, and return, stole horses from those places in the same manner, but to give a detail of the robberies laid to his charge, would far exceed our limits, though he refuses to make any formal confession

of his numerous crimes: he was overtaken with the Cows in his possession; for which he now suffers, and which were claimed by the owner immediately. He said "Mr. Vessey, as he had his Cows restored, would never have prosecuted him, had it not been for the bloody Justices," as he terms them.

He is about 47 years of age; and married Ann Osburn, widow of William Osburn, of South Kelsey in Lincolnshire, by whom he had five Children, one only survives the fate of its unfortunate Father, his Wife had several Children by her former husband, and says he was always kind and affectionate to his Children-in-law; his Wife took her final farewell on Monday last, and their parting was truly affecting and sorrowful.

His behaviour during confinement, and particularly since his condemnation was orderly, though there appeared little signs of contrition, and he said "the bloody Justices should extort no confession from him."—He had great attention paid to him by the Ordinary of Goal, but would suffer no other person to come near him to speak on religious matters, except one of his fellow prisoners, and then his conversation was more on the affairs of this world, than of that to which he was fast hastening. The Turnkey, who is a worthy and respectable man, offered to spend the whole of Tuesday night with him in reading and prayer, which he positively refused, alledging "that as he had but little sleep last night, he hoped for a little comfortable sleep to night, saying, he could pray when he went to bed, and when in bed." Notwithstanding that refusal, he persevered in his kind attention to him, and stuid with him during the whole of last night; he said but little and seem quite resigned, though he did not acknowledge the justness of his sentence, he hoped his untimely fate would be an exemplary warning to his accomplices, which are now at large in this neighbourhood.

At about 11 o'Clock, the mournful procession began, and he was led to the place of Execution, amidst an innumerable company of spectators, who were much affected with the scene. — A very singular circumstance took place at the fatal Tree, when Miller had been turned off about 2 minutes the rope slipped, and he fell to the ground, after which he was again put into the Cart, and soon recovered himself, and while the rope was fitting a second time, he talked and prayed as fervibly as before, after which he was turned off, and launched into a boundless Eternity.

Broadsheet of the life and crimes of John Miller.

alt after only an hour. The Nottingham team decided that the huge crowd was too intimidating for their man and so threw in the towel. Many of those watching the fight were already drunk by the time the boxers were pulled out of the ring and were not to be easily placated. The mob ran riot through the town, causing extensive damage, and order was not fully restored until the early hours of the morning.

797   The Man who was Hanged Twice John Miller (aged 47) had spent much of his life stealing cattle and horses. Generally operating between West Bridgford and Newark, he had become familiar at the various fairs around Derby. Cattle he would usually kill and then sell on the hides, while horses he simply sold on. Caught twice but never imprisoned, he had managed to build himself quite a lucrative business. But it all disappeared when he was caught on the Newark–Nottingham road in possession of three cows belonging to a farmer by the name of Vessey. Brought to trial in July, Miller was found guilty and this time he was sentenced to death. At his execution the rope snapped after he had been left hanging for two minutes. Discovered to be still breathing, he was revived and then hanged a second time. There was no reprieve.

16 August

Old Punishments: The Branks Otherwise known as the scold's or gossip's bridle, this was a metal or leather mask of varying design used to stop a woman talking. It was placed over the head and held in position by straps running under the jaw while a metal protrusion fitted into the mouth to suppress the tongue. Never a legal punishment, its use was essentially a local measure, usually ordered by the village or town council.

17 August

1783   The amazing case of Kitty Hudson (aged 18) excited great interest among Nottingham's medical men. Admitted to the city's new general hospital complaining of being unable to sleep and of a general numbness in her body, it was discovered that she was literally full of pins. Since the age of 6 she had been eating them and by the time of her admission her obsession had become so great that she was unable to eat or drink unless she first ate a mouthful of pins or needles. Over a two-year period doctors removed steel pins from her arms, legs, feet, back and stomach, and after a period of protracted pain in her breasts removed them both only to find they too were full

18 August

A scold's bridle.

of pins. Amazingly Kitty survived her ordeal. She went on to marry and gave birth to nineteen children, none of whom survived her.

19 August **1775** Sarah Lowe and Samuel Webb were sentenced to death for attacking a man named William Ironmonger at the Ram Inn, Nottingham. They beat him to the ground and stole his silver watch and 3 guineas. After both confessed from their cells they were granted a reprieve and were ordered to be transported for life.

20 August **1774** A report in the Nottingham court records details the strange death of John James a month or so earlier. According to the entry, he had been busily engaged in stacking hay, while his 8-year-old daughter sat on top of the stack to watch. In her right hand she clutched a small hay fork, which she had been using to help her father. Unfortunately for John James, at some point the little girl released her grip on the fork, which slid down the side of the stack; the prongs penetrated his head and killed him.

21 August **1794** Terrific storms hit Mansfield, bringing torrential rain, thunder, lightning, huge hailstones and thunderbolts that rained down on the town totally destroying one house by fire.

22 August **1773** An entry in the *Nottingham Date Book* records that a woman by the name of Topli, went to draw water from the well in Parliament Street. As she lowered the bucket her skirts became entangled with the rope and she was dragged in and drowned.

23 August **1824** On this day 22-year-old William Peters, alias Hardy, alias Harding, was sentenced to death for stealing 2 coats, 3 pairs of breeches, 7 hand kerchiefs, 1 waistcoat and a pair of stockings belonging to a Mr James Bailey. Peters was well known to the court and had previously been sentenced to several terms of imprisonment under his various aliases.

24 August **1831** On this day the double execution took place of William Reynolds and William Marshall, both 19 years old, who had been found guilty of raping Mary Ann Lord. Every vantage point in Broad Street, Parliament Street and St John's Street had been taken by the huge crowds that had been gathering in Nottingham since the early hours of the morning. Reynolds died very quickly but the unfortunate Marshall struggled on for many minutes.

25 August **1764** Jilted lover John Higgins (aged 20) hanged himself with a handkerchief from the rafters of his employer's house in Nottingham. The body was buried at the junction of the Derby and Nottingham roads.

26 August **1842** On or around this day some 400 Chartists appeared in court at Nottingham charged with riot. They had been arrested on Mapperley Hills where the 2nd Dragoon Guards broke up a meeting of several thousand workmen

and were merely a representative group. Neither the army nor the authorities could confirm the identities of the ringleaders, and the arrests were made simply to break up the gathering and stop it turning into a rioting mob. Running battles had taken place across much of the county throughout the past ten days. Chartists attempting to stop the progress of industry had attacked works in Arnold, Bulwell, Burton Leys, Carrington, New Radford and Hockley. Colliers had been brought out of the pits, halting coal production, and most textile workers had downed tools. At Sherwood a strike force of some 2,000 men had fought a pitched battle with the military, while a cavalry force had attacked the strike force gathered at Radford. These were dangerous times for Nottingham. The Chartists wanted all labour to be withdrawn, and in order to accomplish that they had successfully gathered together significant numbers of men who supported their principles. Of the 400 arrested more than half were released without charge, while others in the group found themselves fined various amounts of money and fifty were sent back to prison to await trial at Nottingham Assizes. An unrecorded number were sentenced there to prison terms of between two and six months.

1785 The Mayor of Nottingham's mace was stolen from his house on this day. After watching the premises for some days the two culprits noticed that each evening all the windows were shuttered and the shutters fastened. It was a simple task for them to join the household staff. They duly closed up the windows, but did not properly secure the shutter over the window that would allow them entry into the room where the mace was kept. Returning in the early hours of the morning they simply opened up the shutter, lifted the window on its sash and entered the house. But having stolen the mace, they had no idea how to separate the silver from the gold when it was melted down. As they asked around for advice, word reached the police and they were duly arrested. James Shipley was the only one to stand trial, after his partner turned approver and gave evidence against him. He was sentenced to seven years' transportation to Nova Scotia. But Shipley was a cunning man, and when the coach carrying him to the port of embarkation halted overnight he managed to escape and eventually made his way to France.

27 August

28 August **1885** Frederick Hibbert appeared in front of Newark magistrates charged with stealing five ducks valued at 5s from Newark farmer Matt Ward. In his defence he told the court that he had no recollection of picking up the ducks while walking home after a night in a local public house and was surprised to find them in his house the following morning. Whether these ducks were dead or alive is unclear, but the magistrates took a dim view of events and sent him to prison for one month with hard labour.

29 August **1872** After a review of the Robin Hood Rifles at Bulwell, near Nottingham, and an official dinner held in a large marquee in an adjoining field, the soldiers marched to Bulwell station. The train arrived as the troops began to cross the rails to reach the platform. With half the regiment still to cross, the train halted to allow those who had not reached the platform to board. It then pulled into the station to collect the remaining men. As the soldiers pushed forwards to secure their seats Sergeant Major Thompson suddenly found himself trapped between a crush of men and the moving train. Hit by the steps that protruded from each carriage, he was knocked off the platform and his legs were caught between the train and the platform wall. Both his legs were so badly broken that surgeons decided the only way to extract him was to amputate both legs below the knee. He died later this day in Nottingham Hospital from loss of blood.

30 August **1867** Found guilty of robbing Samuel Brown's shop at the bottom of Maid Marion Way, Nottingham, Thomas Reynolds pleaded his innocence. At his trial he insisted that he had not been the man witnesses claimed to have seen. Determined that he should not be executed for a crime he did not commit, he addressed the crowd from the scaffold, telling them he had *not* robbed Brown's shop and would not hang for that crime. However, he went on, he had committed a murder some years earlier. He refused to name his victim but remarked that it was a better crime to die for than a mere robbery. After his execution there was speculation that the victim had been his own wife.

31 August **1800** After disastrous weather throughout the summer many crops failed, forcing grain prices to rise steeply. In turn flour became extremely expensive and as a consequence bread prices rose as production fell to an all-time low. Mansfield's poor were left to fend for themselves and became increasingly dependent upon the benevolence of the rich, who were the only people able to purchase flour for the bakeries to continue operating. Hunger drove people on to the streets in their thousands and they smashed the windows of every bakery they could find. The army was called out to restore order, but there was a further month of civil unrest before bread supplies could be restored to previous levels.

SEPTEMBER

Seventeenth-century woodcut depicting a witch's magic circle.

1 SEPTEMBER **1863** James Chambers (aged 36) volunteered to be taken up in a balloon at Basford Park's grand fête after Mr Coxwell, who was supposed to have made the ascent, withdrew on account of being too heavy for the basket. It was a fatal decision and one Chambers had made hurriedly, having arrived at the park only minutes before the ascent was due. For five minutes all was well and the huge crowd on the ground watched in awe as the balloon headed up towards a gathering bank of rain clouds. Within minutes it disappeared as low cloud obscured it from the watching eyes below. Suddenly a heavy downpour drenched the spectators and, as they ran for the cover of the grandstand, the balloon canopy suddenly deflated. It fell like a stone and hit the ground at Arnold. Chambers was killed instantly.

2 SEPTEMBER **1851** Ancient Britons or murder victims? The question was posed after building excavations at a house in Woolpack Lane, Nottingham, uncovered four human skeletons some 14ft beneath the floor. The land had been sold to build a schoolroom and chapel, and the 200-year-old house that stood on the site was being demolished to make way. The great depth at which the bodies had been buried heightened the mystery, and the advanced state of decay meant that no light could be shed on how they had died. Later examination confirmed that there were two adults and two children. One of the adults had been buried in an elm coffin, the other in an oak one.

3 SEPTEMBER **1800** A reward of £50 was offered by Nottingham Town Clerk Mr George Coldham for any information that could lead to the arrest of the mob that had attacked Edward Barker of the Holme Pierrepoint Yeomanry Cavalry near the Leather Bottle public house at Cropwell Butler.

A poster offering a reward of £50 for information leading to the individual who attacked Edward Barker. (Nottingham Local Studies Library)

Fifty *Pounds*

REWARD.

WHEREAS a moſt unwarrantable and criminal attack was this day made upon EDWARD BARKER, one of the Holme-Pierrepoint Troop of Yeomanry Cavalry (who was following on horſeback a party of the ſame Troop to eſcort the market carts from Snienton to Nottingham) *by a mob of perſons* near the Leather bottle in this town. *who purſued the ſaid ED-WARD BARKER, with vollies of ſtones,* and who, upon his falling with his horſe into a ditch by the road ſide, *pelted him with large ſtones and mud, beat him with ſo much violence and barbarity that he now lies in an uncertain ſtate between life and death, and likewiſe plunaerea from the ſaia Edward Barker all his military accoutrements.*

This is to give Notice,

that whoſoever will inform againſt the perſon or perſons, actively concerned in committing the above offences, ſo that he or they may be apprehended, and brought to public juſtice, ſhall, upon one or more being convicted thereof, receive a reward of

FIFTY POUNDS,

On applying to Mr. George Coldham, Town Clerk.

Nottingham, September 3d, 1800. [Burbage and Stretton, Printers.]

4 SEPTEMBER **1895** Henry Wright (aged 35) sat in the dock at Mansfield's courthouse and kept his eyes tight shut throughout his trial. A lodger at 1 Star Terrace, he had murdered his landlady Mary Elizabeth Reynolds, her two sons Charles (aged 15) and William (16) and her grandson William Peck (3). All had been attacked with a cut-throat razor and their throats slashed open. He had then set the house alight. Naked apart from a pair of socks and a light covering of feathers,

Wright had then run to the nearest police station carrying 2-year-old Robert Stanley Hall still in his burning nightshirt. Police inspector Hopkinson, who answered the door to the clearly insane Wright, grabbed Robert from him and succeeded in extinguishing the flames before the child suffered any extensive burns. Wright had attempted to cut his own throat and was unable to speak, and it was therefore some time before the inspector realised the magnitude of his crime. Arriving at the house, he found fire raging in all the rooms. With the help of some firemen, he found Mary Reynolds' body, but the other children were not found until the fire had been doused. Wright never explained the feathers, nor why he had embarked upon his killing spree. He was found guilty by the Mansfield court and sent to Nottingham's Bagthorpe Gaol.

1757 Riots broke out in Mansfield when the Deputy Lieutenants of Nottingham arrived to enforce a recent government Act that required any able-bodied man summoned by the officers to serve in the local militia (in this case Nottinghamshire). Incensed at being forced into military service, over 500 men broke into the building being used by the deputies, destroyed all the relevant lists of names and forced the men to flee the town.

1828 The mysterious death of one of Nottingham's most eccentric and colourful men was examined at an inquest held in the Navigation Inn after 70-year-old Edward ('Ned') Dawson had been found dead in the canal under strange circumstances. He was partial to a drink but had been sober when he went into the water, and there were no rumours of any argument. No marks were found on his body and no suicide note was found. According to doctors he was hale and healthy despite his age and had not drowned. No one had seen him before the discovery of his body and no one came forward to say they had witnessed any attack on him. His death was a mystery, as much of his life had been. But the inquest was told that the eccentric Dawson would probably have found the manner of his death amusing. As a staunch Tory party supporter he had bought his own coffin some twenty years earlier and as a mark of support to the government he had insisted that the coffin's interior be painted Tory blue. After using it as a cupboard for twenty years, he was finally buried in it after the inconclusive inquest closed.

> The blue-lined coffin holds his dust, now dead,
> In which the living Dawson kept his bread.

Old Punishments: Swimming a Witch When a woman was accused of witchcraft the parish could order that she be secured by means of a binding around her body immobilising her arms and legs. She was then to be cast in water, usually a river. If innocent she would sink, if guilty she would float. Few ever succeeded in sinking. The practice was abolished in 1712, but in 1717 Lord Chief Justice Parker, aware that it still went on in some villages, issued a proclamation stating that anyone who caused the death of a woman by such a practice would be charged with murder.

8 SEPTEMBER   **1831** The *Nottingham Journal* published a report describing the escape of Joanna Ledwich from Nottingham prison. She was one of the few people ever to successfully escape and probably the only woman. She had been under sentence of transportation after being found guilty of robbery on the outskirts of Newark. Determined not to be sent abroad, she cut up a bedsheet, tied it to a clothes line and then, after attaching the makeshift rope to a window, threw the whole lot over the prison wall. Climbing out of the window she then very cautiously began to lower herself down into Narrow Marsh some 70ft below. The knots held firm until she was roughly half-way through her descent, then, unable to sustain her weight any longer, they finally gave way and she fell a considerable distance. Fortunately for her she suffered no serious damage and disappeared into the labyrinth of streets.

9 SEPTEMBER   **1762** Fifteen-year-old Elizabeth Morton, a domestic servant to Walkering-ham farmer James Oliver, was arrested on a charge of murder on or around this date and placed in Nottingham prison where she languished until the Assize Court in the following March. According to her testimony at her trial she had been caught after strangling one of the farmer's two children asleep in the cradle, and during a failed attempt to murder the second.

Above: Seventeenth-century woodcut of a ducking stool.

Her guilt was therefore never in doubt and she made a full and frank confession. In this statement she blamed a man in black as the instigator of the crime. This unidentified man, she claimed, had visited her in the night and told her, as he stood beside her bed, that she must kill the children. Unhesitatingly she had then risen from her bed, walked into the children's bedroom and carried out the instructions he had given her. In a powerful and emotional speech the judge, obviously moved by the young girl's plight, reduced a number of the jury to tears but that did not prevent them from returning a guilty verdict. Unable to reduce the sentence he then placed the black cap upon his head and, despite his own reservations, sentenced her to death. Thousands turned out to witness her last moments, and according to later reports she remained impassive and unmoved throughout.

1861   Benjamin Caunt, Nottingham prizefighter and Champion of England, died on this day in London. His body was brought back to his native village of Hucknall with great ceremony and buried in the churchyard there.

10 September

The grave of
Benjamin Caunt,
prizefighting
champion of England.

11 SEPTEMBER 1664 Colonel John Hutchinson, the man who had staunchly defended
Nottingham Castle throughout the civil war, died on this day at Sandown
Castle, Kent. An ardent admirer of Cromwell and all that Parliament stood for,
he had withstood numerous Royalist sieges in Nottingham and in 1651 had
destroyed the castle at Cromwell's command in order to prevent its future use.
One of the fifty-nine signatories to the death warrant of Charles I, Hutchinson
had grown ever more disillusioned after the king's death and returned to the
Royalist fold in 1660. His body was carried back to Owthorpe, Nottingham in
a hearse pulled by six horses. He was 49 years old.

1882 For trying to pick a fight three times with the same policeman after being thrown out of Newark's Plough Inn, Elias Sheriff, a chimney sweep, appeared before Newark magistrates, who fined him 15s. Unable to pay, he was sent back to prison for fourteen days.

1876 Emma Hewitt (49) and widow Ann Woodhead (73) were arrested and charged with the murder of William Hewitt, Emma's husband. Both denied it. Unhappily for them, they had been seen arguing in a passageway with William on the night he was attacked and Emma had been heard shouting at Woodhead to run and fetch a poker. Hewitt had died two weeks after that argument, but the post-mortem showed his death had been the result of a skull fracture probably sustained at least a fortnight earlier. Despite the two women's insistence that they had not struck him, blaming a fall in the street as the cause of his injury, police refused to believe them. At their trial several witnesses attested to the fact that there had been a violent argument, that Hewitt had been seen in a pub later that same night bleeding from a bad head wound and that he had told a number of people the injury had been caused by the two women. Luckily for them, despite all this corroborative evidence, no one had actually seen the attack and so the charge was changed to one of manslaughter. The jury returned a guilty verdict and they went to prison for twelve months' hard labour.

1812 After two days of rioting in Nottingham caused by an increase in the price of bread, the arrival of a detachment of Hussars and the presence of local militiamen stationed around the city's bakers restored order. Led mainly by women, the rampaging mob had objected to the price not only of bread but also of flour, and as a consequence attacked every bakery they could find and threatened violence against any baker who refused to drop his price levels to those of a week earlier. After the 900-strong West Kent Militia, currently stationed in Nottingham, had joined the mob to protest at the weight of their own loaves being reduced, not a baker in the city dared refuse the mob's demands. To reinforce their message, during the second day of riots the mob attacked warehouses, smashed windows and revisited any bakery that had broken its promise on price. Despite the army's eventual arrival, the mob achieved its aims and bread prices fell considerably in the following days.

1901 Servant girl Ellen Wakeland, after suffering a week of pain from neuralgia, was attended by a visiting doctor, who was unable to cure her condition. Deciding that she would cure it herself, she left the house, walked to the river and without pausing drowned herself.

1766 John Moore, a stocking-maker of Nottingham, attempted to climb down the rocks behind St Mary's poorhouse in order to speak to an attractive young woman. Unfortunately he lost his footing, fell to the ground and was killed instantly.

17 SEPTEMBER **1820** The landlady of Nottingham's Salutation Inn mixed a small quantity of arsenic with some oatmeal and put it in the corner of the pantry to kill the vermin that had infested the pub. She believed it would be out of sight of her family, but she had not accounted for the keen eye and thriftiness of her 87-year-old mother. Coming across what she thought was spilt oatmeal she scooped it up and poured it back into the jar. Later that day the landlady, unaware of her mother's actions, took a handful of oats to add to the broth she had made. The family all sat down to eat it later that night, and her father, John Green, subsequently died of arsenic poisoning. The rest of the family, including the domestic servant, brewer and tap boy, survived only after considerable medical attention.

18 SEPTEMBER **1857** **The Mystery of the Boy without his Boots** A body was discovered on this day in a field near Sherwood Forest. According to police reports it was that of an 8-year-old boy. He was fully clothed and had been strangled, and the only items known to be missing were his boots. He was identified by his mother as John Wesley Atkins, who had been missing for a day, but nothing she had seen or heard led her to believe her son was going to meet anyone, or had met anyone she didn't know. The boy's boots were not new and according to the police had no second-hand value. A search of the area revealed no clues as to his attacker, nor did it locate the missing boots or offer up any explanation

Radcliffe,
Nottingham, *c.* 1900.

as to why they had been taken off. At the later inquest a verdict of 'wilful murder' was returned against 'a person or persons unknown'.

1900 John Bush, a 16-year-old Nottingham collier, was found guilty of stealing a tin of condensed milk, and was sentenced to be flogged six times.

19 SEPTEMBER

1757 Richard Sturges was executed before a large crowd at Nottingham after being found guilty of robbing from a number of dye houses (where wool was dyed). Exactly what he stole is not recorded.

20 SEPTEMBER

1825 Sophia Hyatt, the legendary 'White Lady of Newstead', was killed outside the Maypole Inn, Nottingham, as she stood outside the door waiting to buy a ticket for the London coach. As the Loughborough mail carrier drove out of the yard the first horse reared; its hooves caught Sophia and knocked her to the ground. Unable to move out of the way quickly enough, she was then run over by the cart's wheels and killed instantly. Her body was carried back to her home at Hucknall Torkard and she was eventually buried, in an unmarked grave 30ft from the outer wall of Lord Byron's vault, near the chapel of Hucknall parish church. An avid admirer of Byron's poetry, she had walked to his grave every day throughout much of her life. Always dressed in a white habit, her face hidden from view by a white veil and never speaking, she had walked the grounds of Newstead Abbey from dawn until dusk. Those that knew of her felt it was a fitting tribute to both her life and her devotion to the famous poet that she was buried so close to him. But death did not prevent her daily visits, and soon her ghost began to haunt the grounds. Still seen today, she flits in and out of the trees, head bowed, her white habit trailing along the ground behind her.

21 SEPTEMBER

1882 Road digger William Taylor got more than he bargained for when he pushed his spade into some limestone at Worksop. Believing he had found a wasps' nest he struck at the semicircular object protruding from the ground, but then realised he had hit upon a human skull. Other workmen gathered around and between them they uncovered the complete skeleton of a very tall man. The body had been laid in the ground at an angle, the feet only 12in from the surface with the head and shoulders at twice that depth. Further examination of the bones as they lay in the ground revealed that the man had been killed some hundred years earlier, quite probably murdered. Speculation grew that he had been killed in 1777 because the ground in which he lay was beside the canal, which had been completed that year. Unfortunately, by the time the skeleton was ready to be removed, relic hunters had stolen most of the bones.

22 SEPTEMBER

1824 William Brookes (20) and Charles Ireland (26) were found guilty of robbing Nottingham churchwardens of 10s in copper coin. Brookes was sentenced to seven years' transportation, while Ireland received a lesser sentence of six months in prison.

23 SEPTEMBER

Shire Hall,
Nottingham.

24 SEPTEMBER 1916 At approximately 1 a.m. German Zeppelin *L.17* dropped eight high-explosive shells and eleven incendiary bombs on Nottingham. Shielded by a rising mist from the River Trent the airship had successfully evaded the British guns as it followed the contours of the Trent valley. A large number of civilians were killed in the attack and significant damage was caused to the city. Eleven airships had set out to attack various cities across England but only two of them managed to inflict any damage. Nevertheless, by dawn a total of 140 people had died as a result of the air raids and a further 139 were seriously injured.

Old Punishments: The Cage Of wooden construction, the cage was made up of strong latticework, cross-barred with wooden batons and strengthened with iron. It was most famously used by Edward I on whose orders the Countess of Buchan was placed in a cage and suspended from the walls of Berwick Castle for four years. The cage itself was modified over the years and became a free-standing structure of upright construction. Records show cages were still in use in London in 1707.

1882 An inquest opened at the Newcastle Arms, near Newark, into the tragic death of Eliza Ann Layton (aged 25). This unfortunate woman had fallen off the cart transporting her furniture to a new house in Newark. According to her brother Samuel, who had been riding in the back of the cart, there had been a sudden jolt which had thrown him onto the road. As he pulled himself to his feet he saw his sister lying in the road a short distance behind him. She too had been thrown out but because she had been seated in the front with the driver the wheels had run over her chest as she hit the ground. She died an hour later.

1797 Colonel Williams of the Marines, a native of Nottingham, drowned on this day. He was taking his customary morning ride along the hauling path beside the River Trent in Beeston meadows when his horse slipped as he endeavoured to open a double gate. Both horse and rider fell backwards into the river. The colonel was unable to swim back to the bank and drowned but his horse was saved.

1818 An inquest opened at the Fox and Crown public house in Holme Lane, Nottingham, into the death of John Timms, whose body was found floating in the River Trent at Holme Pierrepoint. The coroner was told that the body exhibited signs of severe violence, particularly about the head, and had been in the water for ten days. A verdict of murder was returned against person or persons unknown. There the case would have rested had it not been for Robert Bamford, in prison awaiting transportation to Australia. His conscience troubled him, and he called the turnkey to his cell and told him he wished to confess to a murder. He then related how he and two accomplices had met Timms in the Three Horseshoes public house. Each man bought a round of drinks in turn, but Timms had refused to pay up. There was an argument. Timms, intent on keeping his money in his pocket, left them all at the bar and strode off onto Trent Bridge. Incensed by his meanness, they followed him and demanded he pay them back for the drinks they had bought him. He refused, and in the scuffle that followed they bundled him over the bridge parapet into the river below.

1694 Mary Kingsley was found guilty by a Mansfield court of living as a vagrant and begging from local villages. The parish ordered that she be whipped in the market square and then sent to her home in Yorkshire within ten days.

30 SEPTEMBER   **1666**   More than a third of Newark's inhabitants had died by this date after plague swept through the town. So long had the disease lasted that the streets were reported as impassable because they were entirely overgrown with grass. A large pit was opened up at the southern end of Mill-gate and all the dead were buried here together.

Kirkgate, Newark,
c. 1915.

OCTOBER

Bridge Street, Worksop, *c.* 1923.

1 October **1767** A strange story was told to Nottingham magistrates by framework-knitter John Shore. Twenty-six years earlier a murder had been committed in Nottingham in the back yard of a house owned by an old woman named Widow Blee. She owned a farm and kept about the farmyard a large number of poultry. One night in September 1741 her young labourer, John Clarke, was disturbed in the early hours of the morning by the geese honking. Well aware that the noise probably meant there were intruders on the premises, he ran out into the farmyard where he was shot dead. No one had ever been

GAZETTE, FRIDAY, MARCH 28, 1890.

AN OPEN LETTER.
To the Editor of *Figaro* (London).

DEAR SIR,—As a rule no one can treat advertisements for patent medicines with more indifference than I do, but I must say that the advertisement in the *Figaro* about three weeks ago so fetched me, that I at once sent for a bottle of St. Jacobs Oil. Of course, I did not expect any "magical" effects, such as were described in the *Figaro*, but still I thought I would try the saintly Oil. For many years I have had stiff knees in the winter, and last year they continued stiff and weak all through the summer. This winter they have been worse than ever. I rubbed my knees with the oil for a few minutes, but felt nothing, not even the warm feeling of hartshorn and oil, but shortly after I felt a tingling in each knee going deeper and deeper down for more than an hour, after which, to my amazement, one knee was quite cured, the other nearly so. A second application, the next morning, did for the ailment altogether. Now how do you account for this? Is it not almost magical? I am relating the wonder to all my friends, and advising them never to be without the patriarchal fluid.

I remain, yours sincerely, ARTHUR J. MELHUISH, 12 Old Bond Street, London, W.

[The above letter appeared in the *Figaro* on February 11th, 1888, wholly unsolicited by anyone. We believe them never with a remedy which has called forth such universal and spontaneous endorsement as St Jacobs Oil. Its effects seem, as Mr Melhuish says, "almost magical." People who have been cripple for years are permanently cured almost instantly by the use of this wonderful remedy.]

A MOST EXTRA-ORDINARY STATEMENT.

To the Editor of the *Wellington (Salop) Journal.*

DEAR SIR,—In your paper of the 20th of October I saw the account of what I considered a most extraordinary statement, wherein "Mrs. Mary Ann Foster, of 48 Greenfield Terrace, Gateshead, had been cured of rheumatism in the limbs in fifteen minutes by using St Jacobs Oil. Now this statement of itself seems incredible, but when the article stated further that "for a long time her legs had been so stiff that she could not stir up in bed," that "the ligaments of her joints seemed to have grown together," and "that her case was considered hopeless," it seemed a miracle which I determined to investigate. I accordingly called on Mrs. Foster for the purpose of learning the truth. Judge of my surprise when that lady told me that every word was true. She said that for months previous to using the Oil she had been confined to her bed, suffering the most excruciating agony night and day, but that in fifteen minutes after the application she experienced relief from pain, that in less than a week she was up and about the house—a well woman. Mrs. Foster says this was more than twelve months ago, and she has not had any return of the disease. She is as well and strong as she ever was in her life, and naturally recommends St Jacobs Oil to everybody—in fact, is a living advertisement for St. Jacobs Oil. These facts speak for themselves of the public, believing that a remedial agent, possessing such wonderful power to conquer pain and relieve suffering, should be made known everywhere. I am glad to see that your journal, as well as the Press generally is taking up the matter, which is quite right. From the foregoing it is quite clear that the Press throughout the country are moving in the right direction, by voluntarily publishing the testimony of thousands of people who have been cured by this most important discovery in medical science.—I remain,

Yours respectfully, THOMAS HUTCHKISS, 46 Napier Street, Newcastle-on-Tyne.

ST. JACOBS OIL ENLIGHTENS THE WORLD.

Denoting a safe harbour where Rheumatism, Neuralgia, Sciatica, and Gout can be speedily and permanently cured. It acts like magic. Thousands of people have been permanently cured of these diseases, after having tried every other remedy in vain.

Mr John White, Consulting Chemist of 97 Masbro' Street, Masbro', Yorkshire, writes:—"It gives me pleasure to report to you the following:—Mrs. Mary Healy, 4 Orchard Street, of this town, is an elderly lady, and one of my customers, who has for long time been a confirmed invalid from rheumatism, and a combination of kindred ailments. To my knowledge she has tried all of the advertised remedies, and has had the best medical advice, yet she remained completely crippled, and suffered the greatest agony. Having known Mrs Healy a long time, she being a near neighbour of mine and knowing her to be completely crippled as above stated, you may judge of my intense astonishment when she walked into my shop one morning, not long ago, apparently completely cured, free from pain and able to walk as well as any one. In answer to my astonished enquiry for an explanation, she reminded me that just twenty-four hours before she had been to my shop for a bottle of St Jacobs Oil. The first application eased the pain, and after the third application she was able to walk, she declares that she is perfectly cured, free from pain, and that St Jacobs Oil is worth a thousand pounds per bottle. The object of her visit to my shop was to request me to communicate a notice to the proprietors of St Jacobs Oil the facts of her case, and to ask them to give same, together with her full name and address, the widest possible publicity, in order that others who are similarly afflicted might be induced to try this wonderful remedy. This statement may seem to many like an advertisement, but to prove that it is not so I will answer any communications addressed to me for further particulars, and Mrs Healy will be only too happy to do the same, as we both consider the Oil invaluable in rheumatism, neuralgia, and all cases where an outward application is indicated.

A CRIPPLE FOR YEARS ABLE to WALK IN TWENTY FOUR HOURS

FACTS.—The above statements are certainly entitled to the most serious consideration of every thinking man and woman. The names given are those of living witnesses. The statements are facts. They can be easily verified. Let the public make the investigation. Everyone will find, not only that these testimonials are genuine, but that ST. JACOBS OIL relieves and cures rheumatism, just as surely as the sun shines in the heavens. It acts like magic. It is simple. It is safe. It is sure. After the most thorough practical tests on invalids in hospitals and elsewhere, it received Six Gold Medals at recent International Expositions for its marvellous power to conquer pain. It cures when everything else has failed. It has cured people who have been lame and crippled with pain for over twenty years. It is an external remedy. It goes right to the spot. One thorough trial will convince the most sceptical.

THE CHARLES A. VOGELER COMPANY, 45 Farringdon Road, London, E.C.

An advertisement for St Jacobs Oil.

rrested for the killing. Now Shore told the court that he could name Clarke's murderers. He then told the judges that at that time a number of soldiers of General Churchill's Regiment of Dragoons had been stationed in the city, nd some of them had attempted to steal Widow Blee's geese. The brave young labourer had simply blundered into them as they were about to leave. John Wilkins and James Cuff had fired the fatal shots before running off. A nationwide search was immediately launched, and Wilkins and Cuff were soon traced to a Chelsea hospital. They were brought back to Nottingham o stand trial but the passing of twenty-six years had taken its toll and any soldiers able to confirm or deny the two men's involvement were long dead. The trial collapsed. Some years later word reached Nottingham that the two men had died – after one of them made a deathbed confession to murder. We are not told which one.

758 Robert Wilson, a former ostler at a Newark inn, had always led a dissolute and dishonest life. Sacked from his job after stealing money from his employers, he simply chose a more lucrative method of robbery and began to ambush unsuspecting travellers on the Nottingham road. It was no rich gentleman that brought about his downfall but a poor woman in the shape of pedlar Sarah Maud. She was desperate for money herself and had no coins o offer him, so instead he stole her bundle of belongings. They eventually led the authorities to him, and he was arrested. He was subsequently executed in Nottingham.

2 OCTOBER

655 Elizabeth Banes, a spinster of Southwell, was accused of being a common scold and her neighbours had forced her into court because of her

3 OCTOBER

continued brawling and 'turbulent spirit'. Found guilty, she was ordered to be 'cuckt in the cucking stool at Southwell'.

1882 At Newark Borough Police Court John Patrick Rogan was brought before magistrates charged with assaulting Eliza Moore and wilfully breaking most of the windows in her house. He pleaded guilty to the damage but refused to admit he had assaulted the young woman. He had not intended her any harm when he burst into her kitchen and grabbed her in what was described as an improper way. The court seemed to show a little sympathy and he was fined 6d to replace the windows and 10s costs.

4 OCTOBER

The Governor's House, Newark.

5 OCTOBER **1913** Just two days after his previous court appearance Cyril Cook (aged 11) was brought back to the dock and convicted of stealing bird sand, string, one lady's woollen jersey, one handsaw, one wheelbarrow and forty keys. The last two items of this list had proved the most profitable for him. Every morning young Cyril had gone out into Mansfield trying to unlock the doors of houses using his set of keys. Every time a door opened he entered the house and stole whatever took his fancy. He would then place the items in his wheelbarrow, cover them with a tarpaulin and push his ill-gotten gains home. This prolific thief was sentenced to three years in prison.

6 OCTOBER **1773** An entry in Mansfield parish records states that on this day two women appeared at the county sessions, one accused of stealing thread and the other of receiving it knowing it to be stolen. Both were found guilty and publicly whipped in Mansfield three days later.

7 OCTOBER **1800** Robert Crampton of Mansfield was arrested after being caught attempting to sell on a quantity of lead. Admitting that he had bought it from a young lad who was known to the authorities as a thief, Crompton was charged with receiving stolen goods. At his trial, despite his plea of innocence, he was found guilty and transported for a period of four years.

8 OCTOBER **1829** An inquest held at the Angel Inn, Fletcher Gate, Nottingham returned a verdict of wilful murder against William Hillary. According to witness evidence, two men, Eneas Simons and William Morris, had entered a liquor shop called the Druid Wine Vault on Fletcher Gate to buy liquor for a prostitute they had met earlier in the day. Inside the shop an argument broke out between them and two other customers, one of whom was William Hillary. They were all thrown out onto the street by the shop owner but the argument continued and Morris attempted to draw a swordstick. Simons jumped into the middle of the fracas in an attempt to disarm his friend. Unfortunately, just as he stepped forward, Hillary plunged a knife into Morris' chest, killing him instantly.

9 OCTOBER **1869** A train packed with people returning from Nottingham's Goose Fair left Nottingham station at 11.30 p.m. bound for Leicester. The night was cold and extremely foggy. Perhaps because of the poor visibility the train halted shortly after leaving the station and tragically was hit from behind by the Derby mail train. Seven people were killed in the crash and scores badly injured.

664 West Retford parish registers record that on this day the last victim of the year's plague outbreak died. No other victims were recorded for the remainder of the year and the total death toll was sixty-six.

831 Rioting was reported on this day in Mansfield after news reached the town that the government's Reform Bill, the first reading of the Reform Act, which became law in 1832, had been rejected by Parliament. Alarmed town officials called out the local yeomanry, sent for the 15th Hussars and began to swear in a number of special constables. A great deal of damage was done to local businesses before order was finally restored two days later. (See 14 August 1839.)

875 Nottingham newspapers reported a great fire at Commerce Hill, where a three-storey warehouse containing bonnet fronts was completely destroyed. Over £10,000-worth of stock went up in smoke and a number of nearby homes in Narrow Marsh were evacuated because the building was thought to be in danger of collapse. Fortunately for all those living close to the warehouse, firefighters managed to prevent the walls falling outward.

Newspapers were the greatest source of information for Nottingham's population throughout the eighteenth and nineteenth centuries.

1902 Mysterious Death near Newark An inquest opened at the Lord Nelson Inn in South Muskham, Newark, into the strange death of James Anderson, a private in the Highland Light Infantry. After returning from South Africa two days earlier he was travelling back to Glasgow on the overnight London to Glasgow Express in company with twenty-six other men and a sergeant. The train arrived on time but when the soldiers disembarked it was discovered that Anderson had disappeared. Later the same day his mutilated body was discovered beside the railway line outside Muskham. According to the evidence presented in court, when the train left London the doors to each carriage had been locked from the outside. The doors were checked again at York. The young soldier had shared a carriage with five others, all of whom claimed to have been unaware of his absence until the train reached Edinburgh. There was no doubt the hapless Anderson had been run over by the train in which he had been travelling. According to the post-mortem results, the train had sheared off the top of his head, severed one leg and the foot of the other, but the precise cause of death could not be

A nineteenth-century Scottish Highland Infantryman.

accurately ascertained because of the damage done to the body. The coroner
wanted to know how a man could fall from a train through a locked door
and how that door could still be locked when the train pulled into Edinburgh
station. Sadly there was no explanation and the rather unsatisfactory verdict
was 'Death by falling out of a train'.

14 OCTOBER **1775** Thomas Hazard was sentenced to seven years' transportation after
being found guilty of an unspecified number of burglaries in Newark. A
consummate thief, he had served time in prison two years earlier for stealing
cheeses and in 1765 had been branded with the mark of the thief after being
caught in possession of 10lb of linen. The judge at his trial told the court that
it was time to rid the town of so dissolute a man.

15 OCTOBER **1771** George Hopewell, a young servant at Burden's Hosiery Company,
Mansfield, was killed as he began the daily routine of screwing down the
warehouse's heavy press. As he began to turn the huge screw the machine
overbalanced and fell on him, pinning his head to the floor. He was killed
instantly.

16 OCTOBER **1776** Found guilty by the Nottingham court, John Stephenson was ordered
to be placed in the pillory at Mansfield. As he mounted the pillory steps he
turned to the gathering crowd and shook his fists defiantly, threatening
retribution to any that dared throw missiles at him during his incarceration.
His threats kept the crowd quiet for over 45 minutes; then, almost as one,
they began to pelt him with dirt and filth.

17 OCTOBER **Old Punishments: Ducking a Scold** Any woman accused of
being a scold was placed on a wooden seat
fastened to the end of a length of wood which
itself was fixed to the ground beside a river.
The seat, or stool as it was known, was then
repeatedly dropped into the water and raised
again. It was last used as a punishment in
1809.

A nineteenth-century
drawing of a type of
ducking stool.

> A smoky house and a scolding wife
> Are two of the greatest plagues of life.
> The first can be cur'd, t'other can't
> For 'tis past the power of mortal man.

18 OCTOBER **1766** **The Great Cheese Riot** After
Nottingham farmers raised the price of cheese
to 28s a cwt people began to gather in the city to voice their objections to the
high price. As a form of protest they attacked shops and stole cheeses, which
they either threw through windows or rolled down the street. In Wheeler
gate hundreds of cheeses were thrown into the street and the mayor himself

Cheapside, Nottingham, *c.* 1924.

vas attacked, and a regiment of foot soldiers had to be called out of their •arracks to restore order. A number of people were injured as the soldiers •pened fire on the crowds, but there was only one fatality: William Eggleston •f Car Colston was shot dead as he stood guard over a quantity of cheese he had intended to carry home.

19 OCTOBER

1773 One of Nottingham's most spectacular funerals took place on this day. The Duke of Kingston, Lord Lieutenant of Nottingham and County, and Steward and Keeper of the Forest of Sherwood, was brought back to his family vault at Holme Pierrepoint after his death in Bath. The funeral procession entered Nottingham at the Trent Bridge, where it was joined by his lordship's tenants carrying white staves, six mutes in black cloaks, a gentleman carrying the ducal coronet on a cushion, two pages, a hearse drawn by six long-tailed black horses draped in black velvet, four mourning coaches, a number of men on horseback and a train of gentlemen's

Robin Hood's Tree or the Major Oak, Sherwood Forest.

carriages. At 4 p.m. the cortége was further extended when it was joined by six clergymen wearing scarves and hats, twenty constables and the vicar of St Mary's Church. The procession finally reached the family mausoleum as darkness began to fall.

20 OCTOBER **1872** William Stevens stood in the dock before the Mayor of Newark and pleaded not guilty to begging outside the Wheat Sheaf public house but his plea fell on deaf ears. Accused of being idle and disorderly, he was sent to prison for seven days' hard labour.

21 OCTOBER **1892** Joseph Taylor was given twenty-one days' imprisonment for attacking farmer George Clarke outside his farmhouse at Balderton after a heated argument with Clarke's wife. Taylor had threatened her but she pushed him away, remarking that he could do her no harm while her husband was around the house. But Taylor was not so easily manipulated nor was he afraid of the farmer. Impulsively he stormed across the farmyard and made an unprovoked attack on Clarke as he worked in a nearby barn, before boasting to Mrs Clarke that he could do as he pleased. The police thought otherwise and so did the court, so he paid a high price for a moment's madness.

22 OCTOBER **1875** Nottingham's worst ever recorded flood reached its peak at around midnight on this day. Most of the south side of the city was under water by this time and the view from the castle by dawn was of a waterlogged landscape that looked more like sea than land. Every house on Nottingham's Leen Side was under water to varying levels, every road was washed away and the only method of transport was a boat. There were several fatalities. The most serious accident occurred on the Wilford road after a two-wheeled cart containing twelve people capsized when the horses lost their footing in the deep water. Six people were drowned.

23 OCTOBER **1822** Samuel Marriott, a Nottingham farmer, was attacked on the edge of Sherwood Forest as he walked along the Mansfield–Nottingham road at Gallows Hill. Three men attempted to rob him, beating him badly in the process. Fortunately for the farmer his cries for help brought two fellow farmers to his assistance. Realising they were about to be caught the attackers tried to escape. The quick-thinking Marriott grabbed the nearest, Thomas Roe, and bit hard into his hand, refusing to release his grip. Badly injured, Roe was taken to Nottingham's lock-up and after cursory treatment made a full confession. What became of the other two would-be robbers is not known and Roe refused to name them.

24 OCTOBER **1872** At Newark Borough Police Court John ('Spongy') Green, a Newark rag gatherer, was accused of using profane and obscene language in a public house in the Tenter buildings, a huge square of terraced houses in the slums of Newark. He was sent to prison for ten days.

Opposite: An advertisement for Moonseed Bitters.

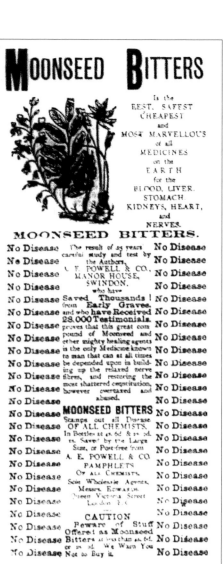

MOONSEED **B**ITTERS

Is the
BEST, SAFEST
CHEAPEST
and
MOST MARVELLOUS
of all
MEDICINES
on the
EARTH
for the
BLOOD, LIVER,
STOMACH,
KIDNEYS, HEART,
and
NERVES.

MOONSEED BITTERS.

No Disease	The result of 25 years careful study and test by	No Disease
No Disease		No Disease
No Disease	A F. POWELL & CO. MANOR HOUSE,	No Disease
No Disease	SWINDON, who have	No Disease
No Disease	Saved Thousands !	No Disease
No Disease	from Early Graves, and who have Received	No Disease
No Disease	28,000 Testimonials,	No Disease
No Disease	proves that this great com pound of Moonseed and	No Disease
No Disease	other mighty healing agents is the only Medicine known	No Disease
No Disease	to man that can at all times be depended upon in build-	No Disease
No Disease	ing up the relaxed nerve fibres, and restoring the	No Disease
No Disease	most shattered constitution, however overtaxed and	No Disease
No Disease	abused.	No Disease
No Disease	**MOONSEED BITTERS**	No Disease
No Disease	Stamps out all Disease	No Disease
No Disease	OF ALL CHEMISTS,	No Disease
No Disease	In Bottles at 4s. 6d. & 1s. 6d. 1s. Saved by the Large	No Disease
No Disease	Size, or Post-free from A. E. POWELL & CO	No Disease
No Disease	PAMPHLETS	No Disease
No Disease	OF ALL CHEMISTS. Sole Wholesale Agents,	No Disease
No Disease	Messrs. EDWARDS,	No Disease
No Disease	Queen Victoria Street London E.C	No Disease
No Disease	CAUTION	No Disease
No Disease	Beware of Stuff Offered as Moonseed	No Disease
No Disease	Bitters at less than 4s. 6d. or 1s. 6d. We Warn You	No Disease
No Disease	Not to Buy it.	No Disease

1817 Jeremiah Brandreth (aged 26), William Turner (46), and Isaac Ludlam (52) were found guilty by a Derby court of high treason after attempting to raise an army to storm Nottingham and were sentenced to be hanged, drawn and quartered. The case was a complex one involving a government spy, sedition and organised insurrection. After the Napoleonic Wars the country was in some disarray. Disbanded soldiers roamed the country-side, bread was expensive and the labour market was somewhat depressed. On top of all this corn prices had been raised to an artificially high level, which exacerbated the widespread poverty of the general population, adding to their misery. Ministers were well aware of their growing unpopularity and the angry resentment that was eating away at the country. To quash any ideas that the government could be overthrown and its powers usurped, Ministers secretly decided to instigate an uprising of their own. A carefully managed affair, it would gather together a number of malcontents, men who could easily be persuaded to organise resistance to authority, and allow them to commit an act of insurgency. They would then be caught and executed as a warning to others. To recruit the malcontents a government spy, known as Oliver, was sent to Nottingham. Assisted by Lord Castlereagh, he was to organise the insurrection here on the grounds that Nottingham was central and therefore key to the Midlands. If Nottingham rebelled, ran the argument, so would the whole north of England. Into this trap stepped Jeremiah Brandreth, known locally as the 'Nottingham Captain' on account of his previous army service. Born in Wilford and living at the time in Sutton in Ashfield, he knew the county well and brought with him to the conspirators' table William Turner and Isaac Ludlam, who represented the Derby contingent. Oliver persuaded them that an army of 70,000 men was ready to attack London as soon as they had captured and secured Nottingham. They chose 9 June as the day of the uprising and Brandreth was told that after he had stormed Nottingham and formed a new interim government he would be joined by a northern army that was mustering in Lancaster and York. He accepted the lie without question. His own army was to be made up of farmers and general labourers who would flock to his standard as he passed each farm, hamlet and village, while at every house he was to demand a weapon. Most households at the time could produce shotguns, knives and even in some instances pikes that collectively would have created a sizeable arsenal. Naively Brandreth and his fellow conspirators agreed to this ill-thought-out plan and began their march on the city at the appointed hour. By the time they reached Eastwood their little army numbered 200 and Brandreth had already killed one farmer's servant for refusing to hand over a shotgun. But it was far from an army of volunteers. Most of those lined up behind him were pressed men who had been forced into service, and at every opportunity a number escaped into the night. So serious was the rate of desertion that by the time they were attacked by the Hussars near Langley Mill their numbers had dwindled to forty and the revolt was over. The execution itself was a brutal affair, although all three were allowed to hang for 30 minutes and so were dead when taken down from the scaffold to be drawn and quartered. The unfortunate Brandreth was decapitated using a large carving knife. It was an appalling end to a sad life.

26 OCTOBER   1814   A rare royal proclamation was issued at around this date offering a reward of 200 guineas for the discovery of the Luddites who had carried out a murderous attack on a house in Basford. Luddites were disillusioned workmen who formed themselves into an effective and often potent force of machine-breakers, capable of inflicting serious damage on any factories and workshops using machinery they saw as detrimental to their continued employment. Basford businessman Thomas Garton was seen as a legitimate target because he had introduced new machines into his workshop. Most of his new frame machinery had already been smashed five or six weeks earlier. But the mob had returned after it became known that Garton had accused one of their number, James Towle, of taking part in the attack. Their intention to kill him for making that identification had been posted well in advance and Garton had employed armed guards to protect himself and his family. Despite this, a mob smashed their way into his house after a shoot out in which one of their leaders, Samuel Bamford, was killed. Tragically a neighbour, William Kilby, had also been shot after he opened his front door to see what all the noise was about. Mistakenly thought to have been a member of the night watch, he was instantly shot and fell dead on his own porch. His killer was never caught, but Nottingham's business community raised £200, out of which Kilby's widow was paid a yearly allowance of £25. Towle was eventually found not guilty of involvement in the original Basford attack, but was executed in November 1816 after being convicted of being a member of a gang that had inflicted £7,500-worth of damage on a Loughborough business. On the scaffold he stood before a crowd of thousands and recited the following poem:

> Oh, for an overcoming faith,
> To cheer my dying hours;
> To triumph o'er the monster death,
> With all his frightful powers.

everal thousand people gathered at his funeral a few short hours after the xecution, filling the streets of Basford.

27 OCTOBER

913 Percival Lucas stood in the dock at Mansfield courthouse charged with he attempted murder of domestic servant Selina Marsden. After a falling- ut he had walked into the kitchen of the Reindeer Inn, Mansfield, where he vorked as a barman, and seized her by the hair as she cleaned out the sinks. ▶ragging her across the floor he then stabbed her in the back and left her ɔr dead on the floor. Astonishingly she survived. Police arrested him within ours and he made a full confession, but insisted that he had never intended ɔ stab her. The whole attack had, he claimed, been done on impulse. While leaning out his pipe he had been seized by an irresistible urge to kill her and ad acted upon it. He was sent to prison in Nottingham to stand trial at the ssizes.

West Gate, Mansfield, *c.* 1912.

28 OCTOBER **1858** In desperation Nottingham labourer John Robert Richardson ran out of his house after an argument and hurled himself into the well at the bottom of his garden. This was no mean feat as the top of the well was no more than 18in across. After a failed rescue attempt his body was eventually located in a half-sitting position in just over 2½ft of water. He had not drowned but was killed by the fall.

29 OCTOBER **1913** Henry Simpson, an insurance agent living at Beeston, Nottingham, decided to take a short-cut home after a long day. It was the worst decision he ever made. Walking along the trackside at Beeston station he stepped between the lines momentarily as he crossed to the other side of the track. With his back to the station he apparently never saw or heard the Tamworth Express, despite frantic shouts from the platform. The train hit him squarely from behind, severing his head from his body and his hands from his arms, stripping away most of his clothing and horrifically mutilating what was left of him.

30 OCTOBER **1660** News reached West Bridgford that its most famous resident, Colonel Hacker, had been executed after being found guilty at his trial for treason. Arrested after the restoration of Charles II, he was put on trial for having signed the warrant allowing the execution of the new king's father, Charles I, twelve years earlier. Despite rigorous questioning he refused to name the king's executioner, taking to his grave the answer to the mystery that still puzzles historians today: who did wield the axe on that fateful January day in 1649?

31 OCTOBER **1901** Newark's oldest resident, Elizabeth Hanbury, died at the great age of 108. An anti-slavery campaigner, a friend of Elizabeth Fry who did so much for Newgate's prisoners, a regular visitor to convict ships, and a total abstainer from alcohol, she had lived through the Napoleonic Wars, the Crimean War, the Zulu War and the Boer War. She had seen out the whole of Queen Victoria's reign, witnessed the political careers of thirty-four prime ministers, seen at first hand the industrial revolution and witnessed the invention of the motorcar. What a life!

NOVEMBER

Matthew Hopkins,
Witchfinder General.

1 November **1785** A tornado, a rare phenomenon in Britain, swept across the count on this day gathering force as it went. It hit Sneinton, ripping the roofs from a number of houses and completely destroying a barn. A witness who saw it approaching along the River Trent described it as a huge black inverted cone accompanied by thunder. Luckily no one was killed.

2 November **1793** After breaking into Bingham's only grocery and drapery shop and stealing 4yds of flannel, some thread, some tape and $2^1\!\!/_2$lb of green tea, Samuel Clarke disturbed almost the whole village with his noisy and somewhat clumsy attempt to escape. Attacked by near neighbours and finally caught by the shop owner's servant John Adcock, he was taken to Nottingham and locked up to await trial.

3 November **1892** Joseph Clarke (aged 12) was fined 2s 6d after being found guilty o throwing stones at Samuel Swinburne's cottage door. He had caused damag costing 3d to repair and was considered by local police to be nuisance in the village. He had made old man Swinburne's life a misery throughout th previous October.

4 November **1805** The body of Thomas Otter was hung in chains at Saxilby Common near Retford, after his execution twenty-four hours earlier for the murde of his wife. The two had been married only a few hours when Otter, known locally as an extremely cruel man who enjoyed torturing horses, had kille her after a row.

5 November **1815** Retford man John Hemstock (aged 19) was arrested and charge with the murder of James Snell by cutting his throat after a failed robber at his house in Clarborough in which he only managed to steal £2 in coin Hemstock denied any involvement, insisting he had been nowhere nea Clarborough. A search produced £1 in loose change, which Hemstoc claimed was his own. He probably would have escaped justice had hi landlord, Charles Lanton, not stepped into the picture at that juncture to te the authorities that when Hemstock had left his lodging he had no mone at all. This he was certain of because he had knocked on Lanton's door o his way out asking to borrow a few shillings, which Lanton had refuse Hemstock, full of remorse, made a full confession. He was found guilty at hi later trial and executed in March the following year.

6 November **1785** William Hands was brought before magistrates in Nottingham accuse of being a horse thief. Caught in possession of a black mare, believed to b the property of Mansfield farmer Samuel Hopewell, he denied the charge an insisted that he had bought the horse in good faith. But he was known t the authorities as dishonest and was sent to prison to await trial at the late Assizes. He eventually confessed to the crime and was found guilty. Execute at Nottingham, his body was laid to rest in St Mary's churchyard after bein left hanging for half an hour.

1597 Mansfield-born John Darrell, Nottingham's very own witchfinder and self-proclaimed exorcist, was called to the city by the Revd Aldridge, vicar of St Mary's Church. A young parishioner, William Somers, had begun suffering from fits that constantly racked his body and the vicar was convinced that the fits were caused by witchcraft. Somers had told the vicar that he had met an old woman in Nottingham and that she had cast a spell on him. Darrell, a puritan teacher, claimed to be able to fight the devil and cast out the evil demons and spirits from any who had been possessed. The vicar thought he was the ideal man to save young William Somers, and Darrell accepted his commission without hesitation. Arriving at the church on this day he immediately ordered that all the citizens of Nottingham must fast and that all men must 'refrain from carnal knowledge of their wives'. Sex, he believed, brought the devil to town. Huge crowds gathered around the church to witness a demonstration of Darrell's powers. He was not about to disappoint them. When the young man was brought forward Darrell performed the fourteen signs of the devil. Then he dramatically cast out the possessing spirit and declared Somers cured. For eighteen days the young man exhibited no fits or signs of possession but on the nineteenth day he relapsed. This time, between the fits that seized him, he began to name a number of women, all of whom he claimed were witches. Darrell was brought back. Within days

A seventeenth-century woodcut depicting a witch with a blackbird.

the young boy's sister Mary also began to exhibit signs of possession, her body going into spasm and convulsing in much the same way as her brother's. Fear gripped the city as the named women were arrested. Then came the first sign that all was not as it seemed. Mary pointed an accusing finger at a woman named Doll Freeman, the cousin of a prominent Nottingham man, Alderman Freeman, who went on to be mayor of the city twice. He refused to believe that either child was possessed by anything more than mischief. It took several months but eventually William and his sister confessed to having faked the whole sad and sorry episode. They had been coached, they insisted, by the witchfinder himself. Their confessions led to the arrest, imprisonment and eventual death in prison of John Darrell.

8 NOVEMBER   1912   An inquest opened on this day at the Brough Wesleyan Chapel schoolroom into the discovery of the body of Nellie Hart, an unfortunate woman who had married a man described in court as a drunken, idle, heartless wretch. He had deserted her on four separate occasions, forcing her and her two children into the workhouse, and had never earned enough money to keep his family from poverty. According to Dr Broadbent, who had carried out the post-mortem, she had died a horrific and extremely painful death from strychnine poisoning. It was not known who had administered the fatal dose since in her death throes she admitted neither to suicide nor murder. The coroner, swayed by the evidence of her desperately poor life, was inclined to believe it was suicide, and after a four-hour hearing it was agreed that the poison had probably been self-administered, perhaps through temporary insanity.

9 NOVEMBER   1811   Riots broke out in villages around Mansfield as the town saw the introduction of new, more efficient machines, which the Luddites feared would destroy their livelihoods. Over 1,000 men gathered at the 7-mile marker stone on the Mansfield–Nottingham road. Determined to show the authorities that they meant business, 300 of them were armed with muskets and pistols while most of the rest carried spears and knives. They descended upon Sutton-in-Ashfield where they smashed fifty-four new knitting frames. Mansfield army volunteers were called out and were joined by seven dismounted dragoons who happened to be escorting two French prisoners into the town. This small band managed to overcome the ill-disciplined rioters and arrest the ringleaders.

10 NOVEMBER   **Old Punishments: Public Whipping** This punishment first appeared on the statute books in 1530. Delinquents and vagrants were to be tied securely to the back of a cart, stripped to the waist and beaten with whips as the cart dragged them around the streets or market square. Once punishment had been meted out vagrants and beggars were ordered to return to their own parishes and if they failed to do so then they would be whipped again. Simple and easy to administer, whipping was well used by most courts, but in time public whipping gave way to the use of the birch in prisons, a practice which continued well into the twentieth century.

A Cure for All Ills Clarke's World Famed Blood Mixture was reputed to be able to cure old sores, ulcerated sores of the neck, blackheads, scurvy, sores, cancerous ulcers, blood and skin diseases, glandular swellings, and to clear away impure matter from the blood. Apparently it was 'pleasant to the taste' and 'warranted free from anything injurious to the most delicate constitution of either sex', and was sold under the slogan 'For the Blood is the Life'.

11 NOVEMBER

Nineteenth-century newspaper adverts were able to claim a cure for almost anything.

12 NOVEMBER   **1876**   Maria Tinker (aged 27), a domestic servant at a household in Elston was arrested after the dead body of a newly born baby was discovered in her linen box beneath an old skirt. For seven months she had successfully concealed her pregnancy and after the baby's premature birth and death she had intended to pay the parish clerk 1s to bury it in secret in Elston churchyard. At her later trial at Nottingham she accepted her guilt and told the court that the baby had been stillborn. Joseph Job, a local surgeon confirmed that in his opinion the child could not have lived. Nevertheless the court showed little compassion and Maria was sent to prison for two weeks and ordered to be kept to hard labour.

13 NOVEMBER   **1909**   Michael Dillon (aged 40), Frank Biggin (43) and Frederick Hodge (40), all Nottingham lace-makers, stood before Mr Justice Channel at Nottingham Assize Court and pleaded not guilty to highway robbery at Beeston. Unfortunately Hodge had already made a statement in which he admitted his part in the robbery, so their defence was flawed from the outset. William Oxley, the man they had attacked, had also recognised each and every one of them. This was hardly surprising since all four of them had been drinking together in the Sherwood Arms at Bramcote until after half past nine. Oxley had been severely beaten and robbed of a silver pocket watch and chain. According to his evidence Dillon and Biggin had held him down while Hodge hit him repeatedly about the face. On the day following the attack the watch was presented to a Nottingham jeweller who was suspicious and refused to buy it; of course he remembered the two men who offered it to him and later identified Dillon as one of them. For the jury it was a clear-cut case and after retiring for only a few minutes they returned with the inevitable guilty verdict. At that point Police Superintendent Harrop told the court that all three men had previous convictions. Hodge had been in prison eighteen times and was the worst offender but the other two were no novices. Dillon had served seventeen sentences and Biggin sixteen. The judge added to their appalling tally by sending Hodge and Dillon back to prison for five years while Biggin, whom he believed could still be 'saved', was sentenced to only three years.

14 NOVEMBER   **1892**   The dead body of 5-month-old Ethel Cregg was discovered in a bed in Basford on this day. Her mother Maggie had given birth while at the Boat Inn in Newark in late June. Unable to care for the child herself, she had left her in the care of her parents while she went off to work in Nottingham. They in turn passed the child on to relatives in Grantham but they gave her back after only a few weeks. By this time the little girl was half-starved and had become extremely emaciated. The grandparents continued to ignore the baby's plight until her constant crying forced them to write to Maggie, asking her to fetch her daughter away. When Maggie saw Ethel for the first time in five months she declared she could not be her baby. It took considerable persuasion to convince Maggie that Ethel really was hers. Back in Nottingham Maggie took the child to a doctor who diagnosed serious neglect, but said she would survive if given proper care. She was sent to a nurse at Hyson Green, but by

that time the little girl had contracted tuberculosis, which pervaded her lungs, bowels and glands. She stood absolutely no chance of survival. It was a sad and sorry tale of neglect.

15 NOVEMBER

1892 John Karnett, a farm servant, was fined the grand sum of 7s after being found guilty at Newark of riding a cart without reins through the village of Thurgaton ten days earlier.

16 NOVEMBER

1825 On this day Samuel Wood (aged 30) murdered his wife, Frances, with a coal pick. The Woods, their three children, an uncle named Dunn and a lodger named Elizabeth Burrows all lived in a house in Parliament Row, opposite Bunkers Hill, in Nottingham. Elizabeth, a new addition to the household, heard screams from the adjoining bedroom and forced open the door to find Samuel sitting astride his wife, who was pinned down. Making no attempt to release her, and in full view of his lodger, he raised the small pick and struck her about the head three times. At his trial the following year he accepted his guilt but told the jury: 'I caught Dunn and my wife together on Saturday and on Tuesday. . . . In all my life I never struck her before . . . I had not the least idea of murder . . . I was not my own man.' His plea fell on deaf ears. Sentenced to death, he was executed a few weeks later and his body given to the general hospital for dissection.

An eighteenth-century drawing depicting the last farewell to the condemned man.

17 November   **1824** Elizabeth Sansom was found guilty of stealing a shawl worth 30s, 30yds of linen cloth, 2 silver teaspoons, 6 pillowcases, a shirt, an apron and 2 handkerchiefs. She was sentenced to seven years' transportation.

18 November   **1866** Henry Rainer, a Nottingham accountant, was found dead, his head resting on the railway lines at Carlton. After a cursory medical examination it was decided that he had not been killed by a passing train but had been murdered and his body placed there to make it appear that his death was accidental. A rich man, Rainer had recently bought a second home nearby complete with two orchards and an expanse of farmland. He spent the working week in Nottingham, returning to Carlton at weekends and for holidays. In order to help with the necessary mortgage he had sublet part of his new house to John and Mary Watson, whom he knew reasonably well. After several days of police investigation the Watsons were arrested and charged with the murder of their landlord. They were eventually brought to trial before Mr Justice Smith at Nottingham. Their motive, according to the police, was money; they apparently stood to gain from Rainer's death. Both denied any involvement and after a lengthy trial were acquitted. The case remains open.

19 November   **1876** Frederick Newbold was sentenced to ten years in prison after stabbing a man during a quarrel. The judge took the view that even though the victim had survived Newbold should not be allowed to remain within the public arena, and ten years was the maximum sentence he could impose.

20 November   **1935** The *Newark Advertiser* reported the tragic case of Charles Henry Sharpe (aged 38), who was found dead with his two little children, Darley and Erica, at their Newark home. All had been gassed. Sharpe had separated from his wife some thirteen years earlier and had been living with the children's mother, Katherine Kay. Theirs was a stormy relationship and twenty-four hours before the discovery of the bodies they had had a serious falling-out over a candle. He had arrived home after an evening spent in a cinema, and when Katherine went to bed, leaving him in the upstairs sitting-room, she inadvertently turned off all the lights. He stormed after her and demanded a candle to light the room. There was an argument and he struck her on the side of her face. In retaliation she hurled a plate and a butter dish at him, which missed, and ran out of the house shouting that she was going to stay with her sister. The sister lived only a few streets away and Sharpe let her go. But after an hour or so he had second thoughts. Armed with a leather strap, he left the children and set off after her, intent on some sort of retribution. Initially he was refused entry to the house but he soon managed to force his way in; grabbing Katherine by the hair, he attempted to drag her out into the street. She struck out with her feet until he released her, then attacked him with a poker but none of her blows struck home. Sharpe then decided to leave her where she was and return home. On the following morning Katherine went off to Goole on the 6.30 a.m. train and it was not until

mid-morning that anyone realised that something was seriously amiss at her house on Crown Street. When the children did not register at school and Sharpe failed to turn up at work police were called to the house. Sergeant Francis forced an entry into the downstairs kitchen and after some considerable effort succeeded in forcing open the scullery door, which had been wedged shut with a rug and a number of empty hessian sacks. Once inside he discovered the children and Sharpe lying on a mattress; the gas taps had been turned full on and all the ventilation holes in the scullery had been blocked up with articles of clothing. Gas was no longer escaping, the pennyworth Sharpe had bought from the meter during the night having long since run out. But it had been sufficient to kill the three of them. In all, five different letters were found in the house, each addressed to a different person. The one addressed to Katherine was stark and brutal. 'Kit, my bitterest thoughts in my last moments are for you. May you go through hell also.' There was no doubt about what Sharpe had intended. The subsequent inquest returned a verdict of murder and suicide.

1877   At 8 a.m. Thomas Gray was executed in the grounds of Nottingham's County Gaol by William Marwood for the murder of Ann Mellors at Car Colston three months earlier. Described by the *Nottingham Daily Express* as habitually taciturn, frequently morose and at times bad-tempered, he was known as 'the quiet man' and was disliked and regarded as dangerous by most of those living in the village. Most people avoided his company and since he preferred to keep himself to himself there had been no trouble. But the quiet man had fallen in love with Ann Mellors, whose mother ran the village grocery shop. Thomas had harboured feelings for the young woman ever since he had gone out with her some four years earlier but Ann, who had ended their brief relationship, felt nothing for him. She had become engaged to be married and had absolutely no suspicion that Gray meant to do her any kind of harm. In fact for the previous four years neither of them had spoken to the other. But on 20 August at around 6.30 a.m., Thomas Gray left his father's cottage, walked through the village, entered the grocery shop, which Ann had just opened, and without warning grabbed her from behind slashing her throat so badly he almost severed her head from her body. Calmly leaving the shop, he then walked to his brother-in-law's house further along the street and confessed to the murder.

21 NOVEMBER

William Marwood, executioner.

Car Colston village.

22 NOVEMBER **1876 The Man who Drank Himself to Death** The inquest into the death of Falkner Hibbitt Osborne (aged 19), a man who was said to enjoy the occasional drink, was held at the Royal Oak, Edwinstowe, on this day. It

transpired during the course of the hearing that on the day of his death he had bought a half-gallon (3.25 litres) of gin from a liquor shop in Ollerton and taken it with him to work. A ploughman for an Edwinstowe farmer, he had continued to work throughout the day, taking the odd break to guzzle from the bottle and becoming progressively more drunk as the day wore on. When the light failed and it became necessary to return the plough horses to their stables, he was incapable of standing. Fellow farm labourers helped him into a barn where he was later found unconscious. He died some hours later. According to the doctor who attended him, he drank himself to death.

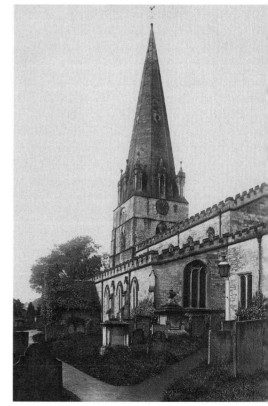

Edwinstowe Church, *c.* 1920.

1892   Servant girl Mary Burton believed she had found the perfect cure for her toothache. Cotton wool dipped in carbolic acid and held against the offending tooth had had the desired effect and so, buoyed up by her discovery, she drank the bottle. She died 30 minutes later.

1891   Nottingham's new prison opened at Bagthorpe this month. Prior to this all prisoners were held in either the County Gaol or St John's Street Prison, both of which were deemed too small and too outdated to cater for the growth in Nottingham's prison population. The new prison was intended to herald the arrival of a more humane system under which prisoners were given more living space and treated more humanely.

1773   The *Nottingham Journal* reported a robbery at the house of Mr and Mrs Topitt, confectioners, whose business was in Long Row, Nottingham. Asleep while the robbery took place they awoke to discover that 265 gold guineas, £7 in silver coin, £10 in foreign gold, a bill of exchange for £70 and a gold pocket watch had been taken from the bureau at the foot of their bed. Mr Topitt immediately suspected journeyman joiner Joseph Shaw, who had been hired a month earlier to carry out some repair work in the Topitt's bedroom. Within twelve hours a warrant had been issued for his arrest and he was found in his lodgings in Parliament Street. He denied any knowledge of the theft but the search party had a trick up their sleeve. The stolen pocket watch had an eight-day timer and had just been wound up, which meant it woud be ticking. A search on hands and knees in the cellar, with an occasional pause to listen, led the search party to the stolen treasure buried beneath the cellar floor. Shaw's unfortunate accomplice William Taylor, unaware of the search being made, walked in through the back door of the house and was immediately arrested despite his protestations of innocence. For some considerable time both men persisted in their assertions that they had not been involved but then Taylor, terrified of the gallows, offered to confess in return for escaping prosecution. The police authorities acceded to the request and Shaw quickly found himself in the dock at Nottingham's Assize Court. Found guilty, he achieved the dubious distinction of being the last condemned man to walk through Nottingham to his own execution.

1811   On or around this day Luddites made a general attack upon workshops in Basford and smashed a number of machines. The Hussars were called out to hunt the attackers down but failed miserably. Within days of this successful raid, others followed in Trumpet Street and York Street, and further afield at Chilwell, Cossall, Eastwood, Heanor and Arnold. In consequence of the continuing riots and attacks, magistrates issued instructions that all publicans were to close their public houses at 10 p.m. A form of martial law was then imposed on Nottingham, with all households being instructed that their occupants must remain indoors after this time. Additional troops from the Royal Horse Guards were brought in to police the streets but they could do nothing to prevent future attacks on businesses, although their presence did lead to a greater number of arrests. Two of those involved at Basford were caught and sentenced to fourteen years transportation. Four others caught at Sutton-in-Ashfield received the same punishment, while others went to prison to serve sentences of between five and seven years.

27 November **1808** An outbreak of smallpox had swept across the slum areas of Nottingham throughout the month; of every three people that caught the disease, one died. The vast majority of deaths occurred in Glasshouse Lane, Navigation Row, St Peter's Churchside and Narrow Marsh.

28 November **1840** James Hitchins, the coroner of Lincoln, walked free from Nottingham prison on this day, having been arrested in connection with certain improprieties discovered after the recent Newark political elections. He was released after the prison surgeon had thwarted an attempt on his life. Bizarrely some days earlier he had received a package from London which contained a large plum cake. He immediately tucked in but collapsed after eating only a small piece of the first slice. Mr Attenburrow, the attending doctor, was on the scene promptly. He realised that the cake contained arsenic and his speedy intervention saved Hitchins's life, though it was certainly touch and go for some time. Later analysis revealed over 2oz of the deadly poison had been used by the cake's baker.

29 November **1826** Mary Ann Darker was attacked between 6 and 7 p.m. by an unidentified man who stepped out of the shadows and plunged a knife into her side. She survived the attack only because the knife struck a bone in her stays. More alarmingly, she was the ninth victim of the 'Nottingham knife slasher'. All the attacks took place in November, and all the victims were young women. None was killed but several were seriously injured and the attacks were clearly meant to claim lives. Despite an urgent search and greater vigilance by the night watch, no one was ever caught.

30 November **1836** An inquest opened at the Bull and Butcher public house, Selston, into the death of Isaiah Brierly. He had been found dying on his kitchen floor by neighbours who had forced their way in through the back door after hearing shouting. In his dying deposition Brierly accused his close friend John Straw of having stabbed him three times in an unexpected attack after the two had had an argument over two dogs. Straw was quickly arrested and at a hearing in Mansfield was sent to prison to await his trial at the Nottingham Assizes.

DECEMBER

Treadmills were introduced into British prisons during the 1820s.

1 DECEMBER **1793** Itinerant horse dealer William Healey (aged 22) had become a regular caller at the house of a Retford innkeeper and smallholder farmer. Presenting himself as a man of property who held livestock in York, he had, over a period of some months, impressed the landlord's daughter sufficiently for her to accept his proposal of marriage. But her father said he would only give his consent if Healey produced some of the cattle or horses he claimed to own. Undaunted, Healey made his way north and returned some weeks later with a number of fine horses, which he offered up to his father-in-law as his part of the bargain. The marriage went ahead and all was well for about three months. But then callers at the farm told the innkeeper that the horses had all been stolen from a farm at Balne near York, and that the real owners laid claim to them. Healey was arrested and charged with horse stealing. At his trial his new father-in-law stood as a prosecution witness and condemned Healey's actions with true malice, his new wife likewise. The jury found him guilty and he was executed in March the following year before an immense throng. The journey to the gallows took a full two hours, so dense was the crowd. He was later interred in St Mary's churchyard.

Market place, Retford, *c.* 1912.

2 DECEMBER **1838** Nottingham eccentric John Wheatley of Lincoln Street decided to have his coffin made before his death. Having no immediate use for it, he placed it in his bedroom and used it to store his wine and liquor. Having purchased the bed in which he would sleep forever, he next set about finding the perfect resting place. When the general cemetery opened on Derby Road he was among the first to buy himself a plot. But his plot was bigger and better than all the rest. He purchased for himself a square piece of ground, about the width of three graves, and had it enclosed. He then

HEALTH FOR ALL!!!

HOLLOWAY'S PILLS

Purify the Blood, correct all Disorders of the
LIVER, STOMACH, KIDNEYS, AND BOWELS.
They invigorate and restore to health Debilitated Constitutions,
And are invaluable in **COMPLAINTS** incidental to **FEMALES** of all ages. For Children and the aged they are priceless.

Manufactured only at 78, New Oxford Street, London,
And sold by all Medicine Vendors throughout the World.
N.B.—Advice Gratis, at the above address, daily, between the hours of 11 and 4, or by letter.

POWELL'S BALSAM OF ANISEED.

TRADE MARK.

POWELL'S Balsam of Aniseed

CURES A COUGH.

This old and invaluable Medicine possesses the extraordinary property of immediately relieving Coughs, Colds, Hoarseness, Difficulty of Breathing, and Huskiness in the Throat, and by dissolving the congealed phlegm, promotes free expectoration.

The unpleasant sensation of tickling in the throat, which deprives so many of rest during the night by the incessant coughing it causes, is quickly removed by a dose of Powell's Balsam of Aniseed.

Those who have not already given it a trial should do so at once.

In palace and cottage alike, Powell's Balsam of Aniseed is the old and unexcelled COUGH REMEDY. Its large sale throughout the whole civilised world proclaims its great worth.

20,000 CHEMISTS SELL IT.

SEE TRADE MARK AS ABOVE ON EACH WRAPPER
Refuse Imitations. Established 1824.

"WORTH A JEW'S EYE"
FOR A COUGH.
Price 11½, 2 3, and Family Bottles.
Prepared by THOMAS POWELL,
4, Ampton Pharm., Blackfriars Road, London.

spent much of the summer sitting out in this enclosure, reading books from an easy chair. As time went by, perhaps becoming more aware of his own mortality, he had a single grave dug out to accommodate the coffin from his bedroom. He then continued with his habit of reading, often surrounded by curious onlookers, presumably content that the hole would be large enough to accommodate him when he died. Unfortunately, when the time came the cemetery officials buried him elsewhere.

1824 After heavy and continuous rain the foundations beneath Nottingham's castle wall gave way and the subsequent landslip buried the houses below under an immense mass of earth and sand. A timely warning about the imminent collapse enabled most of the householders to leave their homes safely but Mrs Millup and her 2-year-old daughter had not heeded the warnings and were buried alive. The mother survived after fortuitously falling beneath a door, which created an air pocket and prevented debris falling onto her head. The little girl had no such luck and was killed instantly.

Above: An advertisement for Holloway's Pills.

Left: An advertisement for Powell's Balsam of Aniseed.

3 DECEMBER

4 December   **Old Punishments: Branding** Branding was used until the early nineteenth century. A hot iron would be placed against the hand or face leaving a mark denoting the type of crime committed: 'V' for vagabond, 'T' for thief, 'C' for coin clipper, and so on.

5 December   **1693** John Walker (aged 15) and his 13-year-old sister Elizabeth were ordered by the churchwardens of Ashmore in Derbyshire to be whipped in Mansfield's market square.

6 December   **1876** On this day the *Newark Advertiser* reported the great fire at Nottingham which destroyed much of Shire Hall, once described by Mr Justice Mellor as the most complete and handsome courts in the Midland counties. At about 10.20 p.m. Police Superintendent Palethorpe had noticed that the windows in the Nisi Prius court were all cracking. On investigating further he discovered that much of the ground floor was ablaze. Nottingham's new fire engine soon arrived and for the rest of the night firemen battled to contain the blaze that raged throughout most of the splendid George III courthouse. The new court wing that had been added at a cost of £10,000 was destroyed and so was much of the fabric of the building. Doubtless it brought a smile to the faces of many of the old lags who gathered in Narrowmarsh and the Meadows area of Nottingham to watch the flames light up the night sky for miles around.

The south prospect of Nottingham, 1749.

THE SOUTH PROSPECT OF NOTTINGHAM

7 December   **1763** **The Mystery of the Warsop Murderer** Arrested for causing criminal damage at a house in Nuttall, John Stowe was placed in the stocks for two hours. He was then brought before Sir Charles Sedley, the presiding magistrate, and confessed to being a deserter from a regiment of dragoons.

Sedley, believing the man to be dangerous, ordered that he be taken to the house of correction at Southwell and put on public display. Stowe, mortified at the very thought of this, declared that he ought to be hanged because he had committed a murder at Warsop and that hanging was preferable to imprisonment. Sedley, unimpressed by his story, nevertheless had him jailed while he contacted the parish clerk at Warsop village to see if any suspicious death had been reported. Within twenty-four hours he received a letter informing him that an old woman by the name of Sarah Wass, housekeeper to a Warsop gentleman, had been discovered brutally murdered in her employer's house, her head horrifically battered and her skull fractured. Stowe was brought up from the cells and again confessed his involvement in the crime; after a close examination of his clothing bloodstains were found all around the hem. He was duly ordered to stand trial at Nottingham's Winter Assizes. There the matter ought to have ended but in Warsop the authorities had already arrested a man named William Barlow for the crime. According to their investigations, he was the deceased's godson and had been seen leaving the house shortly before the murder was discovered. So he too was ordered to stand trial for the same murder. Further enquiries showed that neither of the two men knew the other and they had never been seen together. Puzzled by the bizarre turn of events, the authorities tried desperately to extract a confession from one or both. Stowe maintained his story but before he could be brought to trial he went mad and was removed to an asylum. Barlow continued to declaim his innocence, and on the day set for his trial died in the arms of his jailer as he walked to court.

1876 Strange Death at Gunthorpe The *Newark Advertiser* reported that three days earlier Mary Blatherwick (aged 15) had died at her home in Gunthorpe. The attending doctor, Mr Morris, wrote on the death certificate that the young woman had died from tetanus and lockjaw. There the matter would have rested were it not for a letter Morris wrote later to a family friend. In this letter he raised doubts about his diagnosis and commented that had he more faith in the coroner's court he would have referred the death to the local coroner, Mr Heath. This letter somehow found its way to Mr Heath's filing tray and he immediately ordered an inquiry. Mary had been buried by this time and the inquest decided not to exhume her body but to hear evidence about her death. It transpired after several hours of testimony that Mary had been involved in a fight with her brother on the day before her death over a piece of elastic. In the heated exchanges between the two the boy had knocked her into the fireplace. Could it be, argued the coroner, that the death certificate was too hurriedly composed and that the doctor had missed evidence of manslaughter? The jury agreed and accepted that lockjaw was extremely unlikely to have been the cause of death and that it had probably been her brother who killed her. But coroner Mr Heath, who felt the good doctor had insulted him, refused to summons Mary's brother on the grounds that while evidence supported his involvement no one had actually seen him strike any blow.

8 December

9 December   1811   On this day the bodies of Mr Marr, his wife and child, and 14-year-old shop boy James Biggs were all found murdered in their shop at Ratcliffe. All had been beaten to death during a failed robbery. The robbers were disturbed by the only survivor, the Marrs' servant girl, who had been sent out earlier to buy oysters but had returned earlier than expected after failing to find

An Account of most Cruel and Horrible

MURDERS,

Committed on Saturday Night last, the 8th of December, 1811, on the Bodies of Mr. and Mrs. Marr, their infant Child, 3 months old, and a Shop Boy,—by some Villains who remained concealed in the Yard, till the Shop was shut.

ON Sunday Morning last, the 9th of December, 1811, Mr. MARR, Wholesale Mercer, in Ratcliffe-Highway, his wife, infant child, and shop-boy, were found murdered. This is a most atrocious case of murder, and marked with circumstances of barbarity which are happily uncommon in this country. The barbarous transaction was yesterday the subject of investigation before the Magistrates at the Shadwell Police Office, when the following circumstances were disclosed.

The servant girl of Mr. Marr deposed, that on Saturday evening, about twelve o'clock, she was ordered by her mistress to purchase some oysters for supper, and at the same time to pay the amount of the baker's bill, for which she received a pound note. She left her mistress suckling her infant child, about three months old, in the kitchen, and her master was employed behind the counter, arranging his business preparatory to closing up his shop. She went out and failed buying the oysters, having gone to several places but could not get them. She returned in about half an hour, and found the door and shop closed; when she rang the bell violently without effect. The watchman came up, and enquired the cause of her wanting to be admitted; when she answered, that she was a servant to the family. The watchman then assisted her in endeavouring to alarm the family, but no answer being returned, the watchman went to the next house and related the singular affair.

Mr. Murray, a pawnbroker, deposed, that the watchman acquainted him of the effectual attempt made to alarm the family of Mr. Marr, and that he went to his back door, and was induced to get over the yard wall, and entered the back door of the house, when he was attracted by a light on the landing place. He took the light, and the first horrid spectacle he beheld was James Biggs, a servant lad, 14 years of age, at the farther part of the shop, lying dead on the floor with his brains knocked out, and actually dashed, by force of the murderous blow, against the ceiling. Shocked at this spectacle he called for assistance, when the watchman and some others scaled the wall. Mr. Murray advanced to the street door, when he discovered Mrs. Marr lying on the floor dreadfully wounded, and lifeless. He then went behind the counter, and found Mr. Marr on the ground, bleeding profusely about the head, without signs of life. After witnessing the frightful scene, in the shop, he then advanced into the kitchen, and petrified with horror, he saw the little babe lying in the cradle, with one of its cheeks entirely knocked in with the violence of a blow, and its throat cut from ear to ear.

It is supposed that the mother, frightened on hearing the groans from the shop, left the infant in the cradle to run up stairs to see what was the matter, and that her life fell a sacrifice. The diabolical villains

probably afterwards dispatched the helpless infant to prevent its cries from alarming the neighbourhood.

The watchman deposed, that he was going his round at 12 o'clock, he spoke to Mr. Marr, when shutting up his shop with the servant lad. On his return back, he examined the window shutters, and found one of the pins of the iron cross bar loose, He rapped at the door, and being answered, as he thought in a strange voice, informed them of the neglect in fastening the pins securely. He was replied to from within, by a voice saying, "that all was right.' He then proceeded forward, and again returned, when he heard the violent ringing of the bell by the girl.

The above is the substance of the evidence yet adduced. The return of the girl in so short a time, it is conjectured, had alarmed the wretches, who therefore had no opportunity to rob the premises, and it appears that no property has been stolen. In the desk of the shop 152l. were found deposited in a tin box. On searching the house, a ship carpenter's penmaul about fifteen pounds weight, broken at the point, and a bricklayer's long iron ripping chisel, about 20 inches long, were found; the former were covered with marks of fresh blood. It is supposed that the assassins had entered by the back yard, and had laid concealed there. This yard is surrounded with a wall, and has no communication with the adjoining back premises, which lead into Old Gravel-lane. They must have scaled the walls in order to make their escape after the committal of the barbarous murders.

The bodies of the father, mother, and infant, are placed on one bed in the house, and the body of the lad in the same room. Their heads are all dreadfully mangled, and present a most awful spectacle.—Crowds of spectators thronged in Ratcliffe-highway during the whole of yesterday, and the relation of this act of barbarity, so revolting and so unheard of, painted on every countenance a melancholy gloom. The Magistrates of the Shadwell and Lambert-street, Police Offices are vigilant in endeavouring to trace the perpetrators, and a reward of 50l. has been offered.

In addition to the above particulars, we heard last night that three men have been apprehended on suspicion. Two of them, it is said, were found beside some stacks of bricks near the London Docks, and that blood was found on their clothes. The instrument with which these murders seem to have been committed, is according to the description given of it, a kind of hammer, the iron head of which has a broad flat face at one end, and the other end tapering to a blunt point. It seems that the murderers must have been well acquainted with the situation of the house, in order to enter and make their escape backwards, for many persons in the neighbourhood had no idea that there could have been any communication with the premises in that direction. Hodson, Printer, Notts.

A broadsheet detailing the gruesome murders of the Marr family in 1811. (Nottingham Local Studies Library)

any. Nothing had been stolen from the shop and a reward of 50 guineas was offered.

1872 After a profitable day at Newark market Valentine Peck, a Lincolnshire pig farmer, left his rented room at Castlegate's Waggon and Horses public house to make the long drive home to his house on the Nottinghamshire–Lincolnshire border, carrying the day's takings of over £36 in notes and coin. It was a little after 5 p.m. and of course very dark. He was halted some 3 or 4 miles outside the town by two men who asked if they could ride in the back of his cart. Ever obliging, he told them to jump up and get comfortable behind him. It was the biggest mistake of his whole life. The too-trusting Valentine suddenly found himself facing a pistol as its owner demanded his money or his life. Bravely he refused to hand over any money. The man fired and the ball hit Valentine in the left side of his abdomen. Frightened off by their actions the two robbers jumped from the cart without taking the money and ran off into the darkness. Valentine managed to drive his cart a further half-mile, bleeding badly the whole way, until he saw the lights of a local pub known as Taylor's house. Here he managed to tell the landlord what had happened before collapsing on the floor. Carried home, he was later attended by a surgeon while Newark police were notified of the attack. He had no chance of recovery and died shortly after telling his story. No one was ever caught for his murder.

1759 Executed on this day was William Andrew Horn (aged 74), of Old Horne's Hall, Bellar Gate, Nottingham. He was found guilty of the murder of a newborn baby some thirty-five years earlier at the village of Annesley, where he buried the body beneath a hayrick. The only witness to the appalling event had been his brother Charles. No one had ever discovered the killing and no one would ever have done so had Charles not suffered an attack of conscience all those years later. Having reported the matter to Nottingham's authorities, he appeared as the key witness in his brother's trial. Arriving at the scaffold in his own carriage, William Horn shook hands with all the clergy and told them he forgave all his enemies, even his brother Charles, 'but that at the day of judgement, if God Almighty should ask him how his brother Charles behaved, I would not give my brother a good character'.

1808 Joseph Hill (aged 46), a Nottingham tailor, died of rabies six weeks after being attacked and badly bitten by a rabid dog. Its owner was forced to shoot it dead before it would relinquish its hold on the unfortunate man.

1808 On this day 73-year-old Joseph Harrison was found frozen to death in his own home after temperatures plummeted. The severe frost froze the river water to a depth of 4in and snowdrifts reached up to 12ft deep around Sandiacre. All roads in and out of Nottingham were impassable and it took an army of men with shovels two days to clear any sort of pathway.

14 December — 1909 Samuel Atherley, executed for the murder of his whole family at his house in Arnold, had never denied his guilt. His partner Matilda, her son John, and his own children Samuel and Annie were all found dead in their beds with their throats cut, and there was proof enough that he killed them all. For his own part he claimed to have been out of his mind at the time. Jealous of Matilda's imagined infidelity and unable to find work he had simply gone mad. At his trial the jury did not accept that he had been driven to insanity and the medical teams that examined him in prison concurred.

The house in which Samuel Atherley murdered his family. (*Nottingham Evening Post*)

15 December — 1820 On this day an assassination attempt was made on the life of Alderman Barber. A well-known Nottingham magistrate, he had no doubt created a number of enemies over the years among the criminal fraternity. One of those enemies fired a blunderbuss through the window of his shop with the intention of killing him. But fortune shone on him and despite being in the line of fire all the shot passed either side of him and lodged in the wall beyond. The man responsible then took to his heels; the alderman gave chase but lost him somewhere beyond the market place. A reward of £515 was offered for the would-be assassin's capture but no one was ever brought to justice.

1795 On this day John Hewitt, who had been locked away in Nottingham's gaol to await trial for horse stealing, made a desperate bid for freedom. After forcing his way out of his cell he scaled a wall and jumped down into the prison yard, intending to escape through a doorway. He was caught by a number of turnkeys and a fierce struggle ensued. The luckless Hewitt, realising he was not going to succeed in the attempt, managed to struggle free; then pulling out a knife he stabbed himself repeatedly. The knife was wrestled away from him before he could land a fatal blow, and with the help of local surgeons he made a full recovery. Not that it mattered in the long run. Transferred to Manchester, where his original crime had been committed, he was found guilty and eventually executed.

1924 On this day at Nottingham Thomas Pierrepoint executed Arthur Simms for the murder of his sister-in-law Rosa Armstrong. The 9-year-old schoolgirl had been strangled with a bootlace and her body dumped in a hedgerow near Calladine Lane, Sutton-in-Ashfield. Simms had never denied his guilt and surrendered to Police Constable Alfred Cheeseman only hours after committing the murder. He offered up no motive for the murder and none was ever discovered. At his trial his father Joseph told the court that Arthur had been behaving strangely ever since his discharge from the army, picking fights and often cutting up his clothes and burning them. This cut no ce with the jurors.

1784 **The Strange Will of Charles Thompson** A native of Mansfield, Charles Thompson had travelled much of the known world. After surviving storms at sea, shipwreck, capture by Russian troops, imprisonment by the Empress Catherine the Great, the assassination of Kouli Khan of Persia and the systematic arrest and murder of a number of Persia's governors, he returned to his home at Mansfield to retire. He died on this day. His will stated that his body was to be buried in a field beside the Newark–Southwell road in a simple and plain coffin. His body was to be dressed in a flannel shirt, with a flannel cap and a slip of flannel placed around his neck, and then the coffin was to be closed and bound by three iron rings, one around the head, one around the middle and one around the feet. Eight poor men were to be hired to carry it to the grave and paid 5s each for the work. No bell was to toll, and the cortège was not to travel through Mansfield town. The grave itself was to be 6yds deep and a stone wall was to be erected around the grave site, some 7yds wide. Finally earth was to be carried to the grave after his burial and piled upon it to make a small mound. An oak tree was then to be planted on its highest point.

1803 John Thompson (aged 21) was arrested in the yard of the White Lion Inn, Nottingham, as he stepped out of the Newark coach. He was accused of the theft of a large travelling bag belonging to Edward Godfrey, a Newark attorney who had been waiting inside the Newark coach office as Thompson bought his ticket. The bag was subsequently found on top of the coach in which Thompson had travelled. There was no disputing his guilt, but if anyone had any doubts about it they were erased as Thompson attempted to stab to death the man who seized him. It was widely believed that he had invented the name to protect the reputation of his family, believed to have been landowners in Norwich. Whoever he was, there were moving and desperately emotional scenes at his execution three months later. He had married only two days before his arrest and his wife stood in the waiting crowd gathered around Nottingham's scaffold; on hearing the approach of the cart bringing him from prison, she forced her way through the screaming throng to reach him. The two clasped each other in a final, heart-rending embrace before the noose was placed around his neck. The scene was both harrowing and distressing to all that witnessed it, and the poor young woman had to be carried away in a very distressed state.

20 December **1797** A strange death was recorded on this day at Nottingham's St Mary's workhouse. A pauper known as 'Jockey John', believed to be the father of several illegitimate children, was discovered after being stripped and laid out to have been a woman. Her identity had been kept secret for almost the whole of her life and no one who knew her had ever suspected.

21 December **Old Nottingham Beliefs and Sayings** If you bring yew wood into the house at Christmas to dress it you will have a death in the family before the end of the year.

22 December **1816** George Kerry, his wife, his mother and a young niece had just settled down for the evening in front of a roaring fire. Just after 8 p.m. the door to their Radford home burst open and two armed men ran into the room; pointing pistols at them, they ordered them all to move into the parlour. The women screamed and Kerry made a grab for the nearest man. In the ensuing struggle the pistol went off but the ball hit the opposite wall. Meanwhile the second gunman aimed at Kerry's head and fired. Luckily Kerry ducked and the ball missed, and at that point the two robbers ran away empty-handed. But one of them had been recognised as Daniel Diggle (aged 20), who lived just up the road. Soon caught, he was brought to trial in the New Year and executed in April.

23 December **1822** With no sense of timing the prison authorities installed a treadmill at Southwell's house of correction just in time for the Christmas festivities. Forty-five men per day were put to its use and there were four wheels in all, on which these men had to walk. The two wheels on the ground floor made two revolutions per minute while the two on the upper floor made three. One man stepped off the wheel each minute and was replaced by another, so that, according to prison authorities, each man received a brief respite on each revolution!

24 December **1824** On this day 28-year-old Thomas Alvey was stabbed to death for the price of a pocketbook in the Air Balloon public house in Mount Street,

ottingham. As was customary on Christmas Eve, pedlars often visited the
ity's pubs to try to sell goods to the men out drinking. The Italian Dominic
'atarna had earned his living that way for some time. Well known locally,
e was often seen around the market square and when he walked into the
ir Balloon pub most drinkers addressed him by name. Approaching Alvey,
'atarna offered to sell him a pocket book for 1s. Alvey took the book but only
ffered 2d and refused to hand the book back. A fight developed and Catarna,
ncensed by the young man's action, drew out a stiletto knife and stabbed him
n the neck.

836 By dawn on this day snow lay over 3ft deep across the whole of **25 December**
Nottinghamshire after five consecutive days of heavy snowfall. All Christmas
elebrations were therefore muted and no church bells rang out on Christmas
norning.

Old Nottingham Beliefs and Sayings **26 December**

> If Christmas Day on a Thursday be,
> A windy winter we shall see;
> Windy weather in each week
> And hard tempests strong and thick;
> The summer shall be good and dry,
> Corn and beasts shall multiply.

833 The body of Samuel Kay was discovered on this day lying on a **27 December**
manure heap beside three haystacks on the outskirts of Sutton village, near
Retford. He had been stabbed once in the neck and, according to medical
opinion, it had been quite expertly done. Kay, a Nottinghamshire butcher,
had been in Bawtry the previous day selling meat at the local market. He
was known to many of the traders and had been seen leaving alone in a
small cart at around 6 p.m. When the horse plodded home with the cart but
without Kay, a search was launched and eventually his body was found.
The murder weapon was not found. That the motive had been robbery was
suggested by the fact that no money was discovered on his person or in
the cart. Eager to help, Doncaster police sent their most intelligent and
successful officer, William Etches; unlike many of his contemporaries he
insisted on preserving the crime scene. This revealed boot prints around the
body that must have belonged to the killer. He also demanded a thorough
forensic examination of the body, which disclosed that Kay had not simply
been stabbed but murdered in a particular way. The knife used had been
carefully placed beneath the right ear and then pushed in so deeply that
it protruded into the mouth; it had then been forcibly turned round in the
wound. This was exactly how a butcher would kill a sheep. The murderer,
claimed Etches, was either a butcher or a man used to slaughtering animals.
Within days he had arrested William Clayton, an 18-year-old butcher's boy
from the little village of Clarborough, who not only fitted the profile but also

had been spending more money than he could have earned. Clayton denie
all knowledge of the murder but a search of his lodgings revealed two watc
keys and a watch known to have belonged to the dead man. Etches the
examined Clayton's boots: they fitted exactly with the impressions he ha
taken at the murder site. Tried in Nottingham before Mr Justice Denmar
Clayton pleaded not guilty but the evidence was overwhelming and he wa
found guilty and sentenced to death. Just before his execution he finall
confessed to the killing, adding that he had returned to the corpse durin
the night to steal the money. He had also stolen a pocket-handkerchie
which he had hidden in one of the haystacks, while the knife he had force
into the ground and covered over. A second search confirmed his story an
he was hanged in April 1834.

28 December   1911   **Tragedy on Wedding Day** The *Newark Advertiser* broke the tragic new
that Newark girl Annie Wiles, whose wedding was planned for Boxin
Day, had discovered just hours before the wedding that her intende
husband, Ernest Woodcock, had been found dead in his employer's office
in mysterious circumstances. An office worker at a London brewer
company, Woodcock had apparently left home after dinner on Christma
Day ostensibly to get himself packed up and ready to travel to Newark fo
his wedding on the following morning. At 9 a.m. on Boxing Day he sent
telegram to Annie to tell her he would be arriving on the 9.10 a.m. Londo
train. Inexplicably, he left the station, walked the short distance to hi
employer's offices and let himself into the building. After unlocking the littl
office used by the checkers, he placed his head inside the oven and turned o
the gas. The alarm was raised just hours before the wedding was due whe
his mother received a telegram informing her that he had missed the trai
and asking if she could throw any light on his whereabouts. Nonplusse
by his disappearance she informed the police. His body was soon found. H
had left a poignant note to his young fiancée, but it did little to explain th
mystery of his death.

29 December   1868   Tragedy struck at Bingham, near Nottingham, with the deaths o
Charles Doncaster and a young boy named Attenborough. Both were foun
drowned in the River Smite some 2 miles from the little market town. Afte
the discovery of a partially submerged cart it was widely assumed that the tw
had been trying to push the cart across the narrow ford nearby, which wa
the only crossing before Bingham. After heavy rain the water was deeper tha
normal and it was supposed that they had lost their footing and were simpl
washed away.

30 December   1937   **The Man who was Tried Twice** Retford murderer Frederick Nodde
was executed for the brutal murder of 10-year-old Mona Lilian Tinsley
Uncle Fred, as she referred to him, had once been a lodger at her mother'
Newark home. When he moved to Retford in June 1936 Mrs Tinsley's thre
children, particularly Mona, kept in touch. In January 1937 she disappeared

Mansfield Road Cemetery.

A number of witnesses came forward to say they had seen Nodder talking t
the little girl at Newark bus station the day after she had gone missing. H
at first denied it but then told the police that he had met Mona at her schoo
and taken her back to his house where she spent the night. On the followin
morning he claimed to have taken her to Worksop and put her on to a bus t
Sheffield because she had wanted to visit an aunt there. The police arreste
him and charged him with abduction. At his trial in March he was sentence
to seven years' imprisonment. Both the judge and the police believed he ha
also murdered the girl but without a body there was no evidence on whicl
to make a case. Nodder doubtless believed he had escaped the hangmar
But five months later Mona's body surfaced in the River Idle at Scaftworth
near Bawtry, when the river was being dredged. At the Retford inquest he
father Wilfred formally identified his daughter's remains and suspicion onc
more fell on Nodder. He was duly charged with murder. At his second trial h
repeated his earlier story and insisted that she must have been lured off th
Sheffield bus by someone else and murdered. The jury refused to accept it an
he was sentenced to death, having earned the unique distinction of being trie
twice for what was essentially the same crime.

31 December **1799 The Legend of Postman Baggaley** Heavy snow had been falling acros
Nottinghamshire throughout the day and lay in deep drifts across much o
the county. When mail-carrier Baggaley left Nottingham for Mansfield th
roads were totally impassable for any kind of transport and he was forced t
travel on foot. Conscientious to the last, he believed strongly that the mai
must get through. Struggling on despite the fierce wind and driving snow, h
managed to walk as far as Newstead. On reaching the old guide stone bearin
the inscription

> John Martyn's stone I am,
> Shows ye great roade to Nottyngham.
> 1621

which then stood in the centre of the road, he decided to seek shelter until th
worst of the storm had passed. Seeing the lights in Ye Leather Bottle Inn, h
managed with some difficulty to crawl across to the door and knock. Wher
the landlord pulled it open Baggaley demanded admittance in the name of th
king as bearer of the mail. Unimpressed, the landlord refused and told him t
go and find shelter elsewhere. Cold, exhausted, snow-covered and desperate
Baggaley set out once more toward Mansfield. He was found the nex
morning some way outside the town frozen rigid, the mailbags still graspe
in his hands. An immense crowd attended his funeral some days later. Afte
discovering the landlord's callous action, Mansfield magistrates ordered th
inn to close for ever. The great old guide stone disappeared and was found a
hundred years later in the cellar of the private house that had once been Y
Leather Bottle Inn – and they do say that on a dark night, when snow fills th
northerly wind. . . .